TOWARD AN
ALTERNATIVE
THEOLOGY

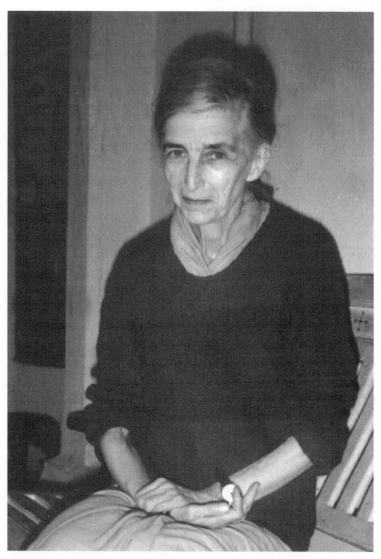

Sara Grant, 1985, at the C.P.S. Ashram

TOWARD AN ALTERNATIVE THEOLOGY

Confessions of a Non-Dualist Christian

The Teape Lectures, 1989

SARA GRANT, R.S.C.J.

Introduction by Bradley J. Malkovsky

UNIVERSITY OF NOTRE DAME PRESS

Notre Dame, Indiana

The editor and publisher express their gratitude to the Society of the
Sacred Heart, Pune, India, for permission to reprint
Sister Sara Grant's Teape Lectures.

Originally published by the
Asian Trading Corporation, Bangalore, India © 1991

Library of Congress Cataloging-in-Publication Data
Grant, Sara, 1922–2000.
Toward an alternative theology : confessions of a non-dualist
Christian : the Teape lectures, 1989 / Sara Grant.
p.   cm.
Originally published: Bangalore : Asian Trading Corp., 1991.
ISBN 0-268-04219-5 (cloth : alk. paper)—
ISBN 0-268-04220-9 (pbk. : alk. paper)
1. Grant, Sara, 1922–2000.   2. Advaita.   3. Theology.
4. Christianity and other religions—Hinduism.   5. Hinduism—
Relations—Christianity.   I. Title.
BX4705.G6178 A3   2001
261.2'45—dc21
2001046428

*The relation between contemplation, theology, and praxis
is an unsolved question of our time.*

— G. Gispert-Sauch, S.J.

Contents

Editor's Introduction

BRADLEY J. MALKOVSKY

The nineteenth and twentieth centuries have seen the publication of a number of notable works on Hinduism by Christian scholars. At first these books were oriented primarily to the topics of Indology and mission, but in the latter part of the twentieth century a sizeable number of texts have appeared which are devoted to the themes of comparative theology and spirituality. The tendency of the new literature from roughly the 1960s onward has been toward a greater appreciation of not only the challenge but also the enrichment offered to Christian thought and spirituality by the world's third largest religion.[1] During the past four decades a new literary genre has also emerged within this body of literature: the blending of Christian theological reflection with firsthand experience of living Hinduism. The most famous of these works have been composed by European Roman Catholic theologians who have taken up long-term or even permanent residence in India. They include Klaus Klostermaier's now classic *Hindu and Christian in Vrindaban*,[2] Swami Abhishiktananda's (Henri Le Saux's) *The Secret of Arunachala*,[3] and Bede Griffiths' *The Marriage of East and West*.[4] Sara Grant's *Toward an Alternative Theology: Confessions of a Non-Dualist Christian* is the latest—in fact the twentieth century's last—in this tradition. First published in 1991,[5] this book is the final version of the Teape Lectures delivered by Grant at Cambridge University in 1989. Here Grant shares her experience of living Hinduism and of its still vibrant ancient wisdom with Western, especially Western Christian, readers.

Until her death in 2000 Sara Grant had been for several decades a well-known figure in Indian Christian theological and contemplative circles. A Scotswoman trained first in Western classics at Oxford and living in India since 1956, Grant established herself as a leading voice in the Indian Church as she sought to promote the significance of the experience and concept of non-duality (Sanskrit: *advaita*) for Christian faith and praxis. But before elaborating on this point I think it is worthwhile to briefly list some of the author's other achievements, so that the reader might gain a greater sense of the authority, both experiential and scholarly, that lies behind this little book.

Anyone acquainted with liturgical and spiritual inculturation and renewal in the Indian Church inspired by Vatican II will know Sara Grant's contribution. She was an energetic participant in countless commissions, workshops, and seminars from the local to the national level following the 1964 Eucharistic Congress in Bombay. In the late 1960s she was the sole female member of the Commissio Technica for the renewal of seminary formation. In 1971 she chaired the Workshop on Evangelization and Contemplation at the International Conference on the Theology of Evangelization at Nagpur. The author spent three decades as philosophy professor at Catholic faculties in Bombay and Pune (also spelled Poona) and from 1977 to 1992 was the co-*ācārya* (spiritual head) of the Christa Prema Seva Ashram, an ecumenical community in Pune which she and others refounded in 1972.[6] In 1993 Sara Grant received the Ba-Bapu Puraskar Prize presented by Gandhians in Pune (the first year it was awarded) for a life exemplifying the precepts and ideals of the Mahatma. Two years later the All-India Association for Christian Higher Education conferred upon her its Eminent Ecumenical Educator Award in recognition of her efforts in promoting intercultural and interreligious understanding.

In this slender volume Grant recounts her search not only for God, but for the right understanding of God, beginning with her childhood in Great Britain, continuing with her entrance into the R.S.C.J. convent novitiate, and finally with her journey in 1956 to India and to its university and ashram life. What we have here is an account of a remarkable spiritual and intellectual odyssey that reaches its goal in the encounter of Christian with Hindu thought and spirituality. Grant thus brings a broad range of experience to the writing of this little book.

I had the good fortune of living in Sara Grant's C.P.S. Ashram for about seven months when I first visited India in 1984. I knew nothing about her when I arrived in Pune, but I was soon advised by a number of theologians at the Jnana-Deepa-Vidyapeeth (the local Catholic theological faculty) that any work I should undertake dealing with the intersection of Hindu and Christian spirituality would benefit greatly by a long sojourn in the presence of Sara Grant. The theologians felt it was necessary that I get some extended firsthand experience of contemplative life in India, and staying with Sister Sara at her ashram was the way to do it.

I had in fact already developed a taste for ashram life only days earlier. Prior to my arrival in Pune to study Sanskrit I had spent three weeks with Father Bede Griffiths at his Saccidananda Ashram in the southern state of Tamil Nadu. What pleased me the most about the ashram was not just the closeness to natural life[7] that the ashram enjoyed along the Kaveri River, the colorful architectural blend of Indian and traditional Christian symbols, the joyous celebration of liturgy with the help of Sanskrit and Tamil hymnody, the simplicity of eating with one's hand instead of with utensils, but above all the spiritual presence of Father Bede, who seemed to inspire a high level of spiritual conversation among the guests.

One discussion in particular remains vividly with me. Soon after my arrival I met an Indian Jesuit novice master from the sacred Hindu city of Madurai who had brought his novices to the ashram in order to initiate them into a more ascetic and, from their point of view, more Hindu way of life (some rebelled at the prospect of having to begin the practice of meditation and yoga). After a number of engaging conversations with this man who had been raised a Hindu and then converted to Christ and the Catholic Church as a teenager (but who did not regard himself as a *former* Hindu), we took up the topic of meditation practice. Here I no doubt revealed all too clearly the influence of my German theological training that had laid such great stress on history of dogma, theory, and conceptualization, for the Jesuit priest offered me advice unbidden but penetrating in its simplicity. He said, "Theology is alright, but if you want to *know* God you will have to learn to transcend your mind." He did not mean that theology or thinking was irrelevant. Rather, he was saying that right thinking about God must finally give way to direct experience itself, and that we must learn to avoid equating the one with the other, and that to attain such a lofty goal involved our learning to understand and control our own mind. This was to be accomplished not only through prayer, divine grace, and a deep yearning for God, but also with the help of meditation practice. Sara Grant, a lucid and rigorous thinker in her own right, would later offer me the same teaching. She taught that while we must never suppress our questioning, we must presuppose on the witness of both the Christian and Hindu traditions that the time must finally come when all thought about God is finally brought to rest by the experience of divine presence (she loved an image from Śaṅkara's writings in which the passive mind is compared to horses untethered and left to drink at the water) and that this liberating experience is possible even this side of death.

And so I arrived at Sara Grant's C. P. S. Ashram. Unlike Father Bede's Saccidananda Ashram, which is located in a rural setting along the banks of a sacred river, the C. P. S. Ashram is situated squarely adjacent to a bus terminal in Shivaji Nagar, a district within the bustling, noisy, and sprawling city of Poona in the western state of Maharashtra. The challenge of daily life during my long visit at the ashram was in attempting to cultivate an interior stillness while physically surrounded by the movement and clamor of the city. If one were to spend even a little time in the ashram library looking out the windows onto the busy Ferguson College Road, it seemed that all castes, walks of life, and forms of land transportation were passing by under the shade of the stately banyan trees. One heard the honking horns and heavy rumble of trucks and buses, the low sputter of motor rickshaws and scooters, the Marathi and Hindi voices of heavily-laden men on bicycles, the sing-song call of women balancing atop their heads broad metal platters brimming with bottles and cans or new cooking utensils, the laughter and banter of barefoot children roaming in groups, the shouts of red-turbaned men and boys commanding enormous herds of black goats or sheep through the city, the cries of fruit and vegetable pushcart vendors announcing their wares, the clip-clop of bullock hoofs on pavement followed by the tinkle of cart-bells, and the clatter of ancient wooden wheels. The procession seemed never-ending until late in the night, when exhausted Pune finally lay prone and silent. The ashram's two watchdogs, Rakhee and Maya, not understanding our need for sleep, would be set off in the middle of the night by an unknown rustle or stir or distant bay and settle into a rhythmic barking that would last for hours. I never once heard the sisters complain about this, and they seemed incredulous at my inability to sleep soundly.

The new day at the ashram began early each morning not with the melody of birdsong or Sanskrit chant, but rather with buses grinding and revving up cold engines and lumbering out into the street. But such a daily external challenge, as difficult as it might be, was actually more easily met than the occasional difficult or mentally unstable guest who might disturb the meditation silence with long harangues directed at Sister Sara, who in such times showed extraordinary patience, compassion, and even courage.

Periods of silence at sunrise and sunset in the ashram were given to meditation and prayer, either alone or in groups, but the daily morning celebration of the Eucharist around a floor altar with attendant readings not only from the Bible but also from other religious traditions was the center of spiritual life. At the same time the ashram recognized the validity of a number of other forms of spiritual practice that the guests might pursue. Yoga students from the United States, Australia, France, and other nations who were enrolled at the well-known Iyengar Institute, located within walking distance of the ashram, were frequently housed for weeks at a time, sometimes greatly outnumbering the ashram community itself. When not at the Iyengar Institute these students could often be seen practicing yoga postures (*āsanas*) in the wide spaces of the ashram library, with sparrows soaring in and out of the windows and peering down from bookshelf perches. My experience was that such students rarely showed any interest in Christian spirituality, even when, as frequently happened, the conversation turned to spiritual topics. But the sisters treated these and all guests as honored friends without revealing any shadow of a hidden missionary agenda.[8] It was in their daily exercise of charity that they most witnessed to Christ. Sara I found especially nonjudgmental; she would allow no gossip whatsoever in her presence. I recall how at one evening *satsang*, a formal gathering given to spiritual discussion, an ashram guest digressed from an account of his spiritual journey to question the integrity of a well-known guru. "Stop!" exclaimed Sara with upright palm and eyes flashing. "We will have no such talk here!"

Sara Grant's rich and eloquent prose, well illustrated in *Toward an Alternative Theology* and other works,[9] contrasted markedly with the sparseness and simplicity of her way of life. She always appeared to me somewhat malnourished and frail, and if one happened to pass by her room it was not uncommon to hear fits of coughing that had plagued her for many years. Her room itself was quite bare: a mattress on the floor, a plain desk and chair to do her studying and writing, a small closet, an aged black manual typewriter, and if I am correct, that is all. But to converse with her was always an educating experience; she was full of fire and wit and helpful insight. I have also heard from others one particular example of her almost heroic attempts at integrity. For many years when she functioned both as co-*ācārya* of the ashram and professor of Indian thought it was necessary to travel long distances across Pune and out into the countryside each morning to deliver her lectures to the seminarians at the Jnana-Deepa-Vidyapeeth. Though no one would have thought ill of her had she enjoyed the comfort of a motor rickshaw and traveled directly from the ashram to the theological college, she felt that for the sake of simplicity as well as out of identification with the poor she must take as they did the more arduous and time-consuming trips by bus, which included connecting and sometimes reconnecting routes. I was told that she traveled by rickshaw only if she did not possess the physical strength to go by bus.

Soon after my arrival Sara[10] invited me to address the ashram community and guests[11] on my life and my reasons for coming to India. This was almost standard procedure for guests, and nearly everyone obliged. At some point in my talk I expressed my conviction that even given the validity of biblical revelation and an I-Thou experience of God there *must* be some other additional way of knowing the Absolute that answered the human desire for transcendence. Sara approached me the next morning on this point and suggested that I might be interested in a series of lectures she would begin to give in the library that very day. I was surprised, to say the least, since I had heard nothing about the talks until that moment. During the course of the next few days I was treated to the thought of Śaṅkara[12] and his teaching of non-duality (advaita). I was immediately won over to the importance of this master Hindu theologian for Christian theology and spirituality.

Like her friends Abhishiktananda, Richard De Smet, Raimundo Panikkar and Bede Griffiths, Sara Grant reflected for years on the significance of advaita both in itself and in its relation to Christian theology and experience. Though she was much influenced in her conceptual understanding of non-duality by the philosophical work of Richard De Smet,[13] in spirit she was closer to the searching Abhishiktananda,[14] with whom she would no doubt have agreed that theology must always follow experience, wherever the Spirit might lead. Both Abhishiktananda and Sara Grant regarded the experience of non-duality as a gift of the same Spirit who was at work in Israel, Christ, and the Church.

The historical origins of the Hindu experience and articulation of non-duality go back at least as far as the Upanishads (900–200 B.C.E.), a collection of revealed scriptures that announce the highest truth of reality and the path that overcomes creaturely suffering. The Upanishads do not themselves present ontology in a systematic or completely unified manner, and so a number of Hindu thinkers through the ages have been able to argue that advaita is not the correct or only understanding of these texts. Such objections notwithstanding, the tradition of advaita experience and commentary, called Advaita Vedānta, has been the dominant school of Hindu thought since the time of the monk and reformer Śaṅkara (ca. 700 C.E.). Śaṅkara is Advaita's most important and influential commentator and his writings have given advaita its definitive theological expression.

Despite differences of interpretation among Advaitins regarding the ontological status of the world, non-duality always refers to the unity of all being in the One. The world in all its multiplicity is never "outside" or external to its infinite simple Source nor can the two be added up as if they were entities in a series. The world exists by participation in the supremely Real, so that it may be said that while the two—the world and its Source—are distinct, they are not realities set apart. The Upanishads speak here of an experience of the Absolute (*brahman*) not as Object or Thou, but as supreme immanent Subject or Self (*ātman*). In the face of this overwhelming experience of the all-pervasiveness of the Eternal, everything finite appears relativized, even threatened with obliteration, including one's own individual human importance. As an *idea* thus described, advaita can be quickly dispensed with by Christian theology as false or heretical, since it seems to deny an ultimate significance to the world, but as a living *experience* its truth is unshakeable and impossible to ignore. People such as Abhishiktananda and Sara Grant staked their whole existence on reconciling the truth of Christian revelation with the experience of non-duality.

What is special about Sara Grant's odyssey is that a dim awareness of the non-dual nature of reality manifested itself already in childhood as a problem to be solved, and her Christian upbringing offered her nothing that might make sense of that perception or integrate it into the Christian vision of life. It was only later, in her reading of Aquinas and Śaṅkara in a method of mutual illumination, that she was to discover how the advaitic insight was quite compatible with Catholic theology. She began to realize how non-dualistic teaching is present, though underdeveloped, in authentic Christian doctrine. At the same time, it is true, Christian revelation gives a value to the world and offers a final eschatological hope that is generally lacking in Advaita Vedānta. But the purpose of Sara Grant's book is not to show what Christianity has to offer Hinduism, but rather to elucidate how Christian theology and spirituality might be enriched by the encounter with advaita. It was her conviction that a right understanding of non-duality could serve as an important corrective to much widespread popular Christian misconception about God and creation. But it is important to leave the telling of that story to Sara Grant herself, who writes out of experience and deep reflection and with great eloquence.

Notes

1. Hinduism, or rather a collection of religions that in modern times goes by the name of Hinduism, is third after Christianity and Islam. It is numerically greater than any of the other Asian religions, for instance, Buddhism, Confucianism, and Taoism; there are perhaps as many as 800 million Hindus today.

2. Klaus Klostermaier, *Hindu and Christian in Vrindaban* (London: SCM Press, 1993; first published in 1969). Klostermaier is originally from Germany but now resides in Canada.

3. Swami Abhishiktananda, *The Secret of Arunachala* (Delhi: ISPCK, 1979). Abhishiktananda was from France.

4. Bede Griffiths, *The Marriage of East and West* (Springfield, Ill.: Templegate, 1982). Griffiths was a native of Great Britain. Other important European Christian theologian-Indologists of Sara Grant's generation, but with a less autobiographical bent, are Raimundo Panikkar (Spain) and Richard De Smet (Belgium). Diana Eck, an American Methodist and Indologist at Harvard, has recently included many anecdotes of her meetings and friendships with Hindus in India in her *Encountering God* (Boston: Beacon Press, 1993).

5. Sara Grant, *Towards an Alternative Theology: Confessions of a Non-Dualist Christian* (Bangalore: Asian Trading Corporation, 1991).

6. The C.P.S. Ashram was originally established in 1927 and enjoyed the friendship of and a number of visits by Mohandas Gandhi.

7. It was not uncommon to see peacocks strutting in and out of the chapel in the daytime, and to hear them screeching from atop the palm trees at night. I received an unexpected visit on my very first night at the ashram when I awoke to find a large rat perched beside my head on the pillow. I also heard reports that cobras had been spotted in the thatched roofs of the monks' quarters, and that they never posed any serious threat to human life.

8. But if the issue of Christ or Church were to emerge the sisters were quite prepared to explain their convictions.

9. See also Sara Grant's "Śaṅkara's Concept of Śruti as a Pramāṇa," in *Research Seminar on Non-Biblical Scriptures*, ed. D.S. Amalorpavadass (Bangalore: National Biblical, Catechetical and Liturgical Centre, 1974), 340–359; "Christian Theologizing and the Challenge of Advaita," in

Theologizing in India, ed. M. Amaladoss et al. (Bangalore: Theological Publications of India, 1981), 70–80; *Lord of the Dance* (Bangalore: Asian Trading Corporation, 1987); and *Śaṅkarācārya's Concept of Relation* (Delhi: Motilal Banarsidass, 1999).

10. She, like most of the other sisters, preferred to be addressed by the familiar first name rather than by the more distancing "Sister."

11. Here the yoga students were frequent visitors, for what interested them most was the life experience reported by others.

12. Pronounced SHAHN-ka-ra.

13. De Smet was the unofficial guide of Grant's dissertation, "The Concept of Relation in Śaṅkarāchārya" (University of Bombay, 1972), revised for publication in 1999 (see note 9 above). For more on De Smet see my "The Life and Work of Richard De Smet, S.J.," in *New Perspectives on Advaita Vedānta: Essays in Commemoration of Richard De Smet,* ed. Bradley J. Malkovsky (Leiden: E.J. Brill, 2000), 1–17.

14. For a comparison of the approaches of Abhishiktananda and De Smet to Advaita Vedānta see my "Advaita Vedānta and Christian Faith," *Journal of Ecumenical Studies* 36 (1999): 397–422.

Foreword

URSULA KING

It was a great pleasure to receive Sister Sara Grant in 1989 to give the distinguished Teape Lectures in England. The main venue for these lectures was the University of Cambridge, but we were fortunate at the University of Bristol to have the lectures given there as well. I had arrived in Bristol only a few months earlier and was particularly pleased to welcome Sister Sara as the first guest in my new home after we had last met quite some years ago at a conference in India. Besides discussing her lectures we shared many thoughts about Indian spirituality and Hindu-Christian dialogue, and I learnt much about life in the Christa Prema Seva Ashram in Pune, which I have not had the good fortune yet to have visited; since our discussions my wish to go there has grown very strong indeed.

Sister Sara's lectures were deeply personal and most rewarding to discerning listeners eager to learn about the Indian experience of a Scottish sister who had lived a large part of her life in contact with Hindus and was thereby so transformed that she could share with us the "confessions of a non-dualist Christian." Drawing on her rich Christian and Indian experiences, Sister Sara expresses in these lectures subtle and thought-provoking attempts to find an alternative theology in which the perennial human search for union and ultimate oneness,

xxi

the unfathomable mystery that is Reality, is expressed in refreshingly personal terms.

In her first lecture she describes her personal spiritual quest whose roots reach far back into her childhood, a quest for oneness so deep and compelling that she speaks of herself as a "natural non-dualist." Her passionate emotional and intellectual need for clarity and the order of a unifying vision which links outer forms and teaching to inner experience are strongly expressed in the synthesis outlined in the following pages. Here ideas and experiences from our Eastern and Western spiritual heritage are combined; yet their very expression also points beyond the barriers of all language toward a Reality which ultimately transcends the divisions of our geographical, cultural, and religious differences.

The second lecture vividly describes the challenge of Advaita which Sister Sara encountered during her life and work in India, and in the third lecture this challenge is integrated with a new and deeper understanding of Christianity, much of which, through her work in communion with that of others, is embodied in the life and activities of the Christa Prema Seva Ashram in Pune. This and other examples given from much larger areas of activity are a living proof that the author of these lectures is not content with merely theologizing as a purely mental exercise arising from an alternative life experience; they demonstrate her concern and compassion by exemplifying a theologizing into an alternative praxis, what she calls "non-dualism in action."

Sister Sara's lectures pose a series of challenging questions which readers will have to ponder in their own minds and hearts — questions for Christians concerned to discover and encounter in depth some of the rich dimensions of the Hindu spiritual heritage. Her reflections also call into question some of the narrowness of the "Latin bondage" of much of Western institutional Christianity and its rigidified doctrines, which at times can appear devoid of the life of the spirit.

I warmly recommend this book to anyone interested in Hindu-Christian dialogue as an in-depth encounter of great enrichment, and in fact to anyone who wishes to feel and taste a living spirituality that can nourish, guide, and transform life in action.

Acknowledgments

I wish to record here my deep gratitude to the Trustees and Cambridge Committee of the Teape Foundation for inviting me to give the Teape Lectures for 1989, for their warm hospitality and encouragement, and for their generous contribution toward publication of the lectures.

I am also greatly indebted to Dr. Ursula King, Head of the Department of Theology and Religious Studies in the University of Bristol, for her invitation to repeat the lectures at the Ecumenical Centre there, for giving me the freedom of her home, and for the friendship which led her to agree so willingly to write the foreword for this book.

I hope that the lectures as they appear here will be recognizable to those who heard them: the present text formed, as it were, the ground-base for the verbal presentation. I have altered very little, except to put rather more order and discipline into the third lecture. It seemed pointless to attempt to impose an appearance of finality on something which had from the beginning declared itself to be and still remains an ongoing quest.

To all who have shared in that quest and in the labour of publication — the Indian and English Provinces of the Society of the Sacred Heart, my own ashram community, and the many guests who have contributed over the years to our experience and our reflection, formal and informal, and those in Cambridge and Bristol with whom such tangible and deep bonds of friendship were so swiftly formed — I offer these tentative gropings of gratitude and love.

Sara Grant, R.S.C.J.
Christa Prema Seva Ashram, Pune
September 17, 1990

Preliminary Remarks

I feel I must begin with an expression of gratitude to the
Teape Foundation for giving me the opportunity to think and
speak about something which has been a perpetual and
increasingly dominating preoccupation of mine for over thirty
years—namely, the implications of the Hindu experience of
non-duality for Christian theological reflection. In 1983, in one
of my last conversations with him, that wise Scottish Jesuit
and man of God Lachlan Hughes had already urged me to
write something autobiographical and theological about my
experience of being reborn, as it were, into a totally different
cultural and religious situation, and the transformation this,
and especially my study of Śaṅkarācārya, the great ninth-
century Hindu theologian, had brought about in me and my
worldview, particularly in my understanding of the mystery
of Christ. A number of others whose opinion I respect told me,
some with considerable vigor, that I should act on his sugges-
tion, so when the invitation came to give the Teape lectures
there was no need to search for a subject.

Perhaps I should also say something about the spirit in which
these reflections are offered, which is that of a thinking-aloud, a
shared search, not a didactic presentation of oracular certain-
ties. I also want to state clearly that I do not believe in the simplistic distinction sometimes made between the active, extrovert,
uncontemplative West and the spiritual East. My experience of

1

human nature as it is found in all of us, whether Eastern or Western by birth, is perhaps best illustrated by the beautiful image of the *Ardnāri,* Lord Śiva represented as one human figure, half-man, half-woman, an image reflected in Jung's conception of the animus and anima, present in varying degrees in both sexes, issuing ideally in a relation of mutually respectful complementarity in which each recognizes something of the other in themselves, and so perhaps is enabled to correct any imbalance in their own way of being.

This is where autobiography becomes relevant, for I think my going to India brought to full awareness in me a fundamental way of being and thinking which I had hitherto experienced as a rather uncomfortable, obscure, and unorthodox genetic twist (there was nothing in my upbringing to account for it) and gave it a specific context and respectability in the age-old Hindu classification of spiritual paths based on temperament and the predominance of the natural drawing to *jñāna* or wisdom, *bhakti* or loving devotion, and *karma* or devoted service.

The significance of this in the present context is that it underlines the truth that non-dualists are not confined to the East, though perhaps they are less common in the West, at least in an extreme form. In fact, in accepting the invitation to give these lectures I was partly motivated by the hope that they might find an echo in the heart of at least a few other crypto non-dualists and so help them to recognize their own identity and come to terms with it, and also, especially if they were from a Christian background, help them to recognize and relate to the ultimate non-dualism of Christian revelation.

I say "ultimate non-dualism," for every human being in the body, and every society of human beings, including the Churches, necessarily has elements of *jñāni, bhakti,* and *karma.* We are all intelligent creatures capable of "knowledge of things in their ultimate cause," in Aristotle's phrase defining wisdom, capable too of affective relationships and self-directed action.

Most of us are therefore very comfortable most of the time with a dualistic worldview of I and thou, subject and object, for we are other-oriented from birth; as the Upanishads say, "man's Maker pierced the holes of his senses outward," so human beings naturally look without, but, they add, "some wise man, desiring immortality, looked within and found the Self." "Immortality" here does not mean endless life on the present plane of existence, but rather means awareness of another dimension of being, of the Eternal in the fleeting Now of time, that "point of intersection between the Timeless and time," as T. S. Eliot puts it. Some glimpse of this and its staggering implications probably comes to every human being, however fleetingly, at least once in a lifetime: for many I think it remains as a kind of background music, hardly adverted to, but always there at the back of the mind. To be pursued by this awareness with the relentless persistence of the Eumenides is the crucifying and liberating lot of the typical *jñāni* or non-dualist.

It is, I think, the apparent inability of the Churches to meet the challenge of this depth-dimension of human existence which largely accounts for their loss of credibility today in the eyes of many profoundly serious and spiritual men and women, however much they may appreciate Church initiatives in the fields of, for example, justice and social action. It seems to be too easily forgotten, if indeed it is realized at all, that catering to man's deep inner hunger is also a part of justice.

I hope, then, to show, as my overall title "Toward an Alternative Theology" suggests, that the basic intuition of non-dualism as we find it in the Upanishads and the great commentaries of Śaṅkarācārya has immensely exciting possibilities for us today as we search for a common basis for cross-cultural attempts to make sense of our experience as humans and Christians on the earth, besieged by all the pluralisms and apparent dichotomies of our common condition. To me, living as I do in an interreligious community which has been described as "a crossroads of the Spirit," the theological, or perhaps I should say metatheological, possibilities in the field of religious pluralism are especially exhilarating. I cannot, on the basis of my experience of the past thirty years, accept the view put forward by many that we must in the end accept a relativist juxtaposition of religions, each offering their own ultimate vision, with no discernible relation or harmony between them. And yet clearly the exclusive and triumphalist attitudes of the past cannot lawfully be revived, or propagated where they still exist. Here too, I think, non-dualism may offer a key to a situation which it reveals as intrinsically intolerable.

One final point I should mention: some might very understandably question the competence of a Christian to offer a valid interpretation of one of the great traditions of Hinduism, as Christians would question the competence of a Hindu to interpret the Gospel. It may therefore be in order to say that although some Hindu scholars who are still mistrustful of modern methods of textual study and exegesis would not be open to the interpretation given here, I have several times been deeply humbled by the openness with which it has been accepted in Hindu circles. In the Sivananda Ashram in Rishikesh I was asked to speak at the evening *satsang* on Śaṅkara's concept of relation, and the presiding Swamiji told me at the end that it was extraordinary and almost unbelievable that a Christian should have such an understanding of Śaṅkara. I had a similar experience in the Sri Ramana Ashram at Tiruvannamalai with the cousin of Ramana Maharshi, and in the nearby Tapovanam Ashram with a disciple of Gnanananda, the Guru of Abhishiktananda's *Guru and Disciple*. In philosophical circles in India, Father R. V. De Smet, S.J., to whom I am greatly indebted, has long been respected as a pioneer and authority in this field, and it is increasingly coming to be recognized even in scholarly Hindu circles that a return to the sources does indeed reveal a rather different Śaṅkara from the elusive "world-negating pessimist" of the university text-book and popular opinion.

LECTURE 1

The Questing Beast:
Mainly Autobiographical

A quest that searches even for its own formulation.
— G. Gispert-Sauch, *Bliss in the Upanishads*

I see well that our intellect is never sated unless that True enlightens it outside of which no truth has space. In that it reposes, like a beast in its lair, as soon as it gains it; and gain it it can, else every desire were in vain. Because of this doubt springs up like a shoot at the foot of truth, and it is nature itself which urges us to the summit, from height to height.
—Dante, *Paradiso* 4.129–132

After living in India for some time I realized that I had been a non-dualist from birth. Perhaps the simplest way to explain what I mean by this is to give an example: Imagine a man standing in a field, only the man and his shadow. If you asked a group of people how many things were in the field, some might say one, some might say two—only the man, or the man and his shadow. The non-dualists would argue for the reality of the shadow, but they could not deny its dependence on the man. The crux of the question is the nature of the relation between man and shadow.

Another example: my spontaneous reaction to an article by Father William Barry, S.J., in *The Tablet* (7 June 1989) called

"The Dance of God," in which he stated that the "I-Thou" paradigm offers "the only appropriate language" for expressing our relation to God. I felt constrained to point out that, in India at least, this is not the case, for

> in the non-dualist tradition of Hinduism, and in much of Sufism also, the language of "I" and "Thou" has been to many a source of intolerable anguish, however naturally it may come to most of us in our embodied state, because it seems to run counter to a profound metaphysical impulse for a depth of union which transcends all subject-object dichotomy, and yet is emphatically not pantheistic: the supreme Mystery is experienced as the Self of one's own self ("I live now no longer I . . ."). This tension is admirably expressed by the late-medieval Hindu saint Sadashiva, in describing his own attempt to use the "I-Thou" formula in his prayer: "I can find no corner within my heart where I may take my stand to worship him, *for in every 'I' which I attempt to utter, his 'I' is already glowing.*" (Letter to *The Tablet*, 29 July 1989)

I cannot claim that I was clearly aware of this dilemma from the dawn of reason, but when I first came across Sadashiva's cry of desperation some years after my arrival in India, I knew exactly what he meant, and it made sense of all the nameless discomfort that had bedeviled my own search from very early years. My worldview was formed from childhood in the traditional Christian mold, based on the at least apparently dualistic vision of the Bible: the first three chapters of Genesis exerted a magnetic attraction on my eldest brother and me. When I was three years old we knew them practically by heart and never tired of hearing them read. They made good sense to us, for our own home was based firmly and lovingly on the same assumptions of a God who had created man and given him commands and prohibitions for his own good, disobedience to which could have no healthy consequences. Even the most radical non-dualists recognize that the world of ordinary experience is made up of a balance of "pairs of opposites": night and day, light and darkness, good and evil, nice and nasty, girl and boy, and I had no difficultly in accepting this, or the dependence of everything on "God up there." It was only gradually that I became aware of a sense of somehow living in two dimensions of consciousness, that of the visible world of everyday life, and that of another, mysterious world, least inadequately described as the sense of a presence which was also an absence, a rather crude way of expressing the transcendence-in-immanence which characterizes the non-dualist position as distinct from that of the absolute monist, who makes no real distinction between the Eternal and its created manifestation.

What baffled me more and more was that no one else seemed to be bothered by this awareness of two dimensions of being and the need to reconcile them. We were given very practical basic religious formation by my mother, and at the age of eight I was sent to the Convent of the Sacred Heart, Roehampton (the "Convent of the Five Wounds" of the novel "Frost in May") to be prepared for my first sacramental communion. I must confess that although this was for me an extraordinary and decisive experience, this was more the result of something in the atmosphere of the place than of the actual instruction we were given, which somehow did not seem to be related in any way to my inner sense of all-enveloping yet intangible Presence. As far as I remember, much stress was put on the "first coming of Jesus into my soul," but it was all expressed in rather concrete and "solid" terms without, I think, sufficient advertence to the very strong sense of the mystery and omnipresence of God which I am convinced is the birthright of all young children in their natural state, and no reference whatever—again, so far as I remember—to the fact that God was already in my soul. Anyway, the little "cat that walked by itself" inside was not really touched by the names and forms offered it as means of expression—the grid did not fit, so much so that years afterwards my mother told me that she thought I had been exposed too young to the experience. I do not think so; something tremendous had happened at a very deep level that defied verbal expression. When someone asked me twenty years later about the origins of my religious vocation, I realized that it was during these weeks that I had first understood that it was possible to live with other people and yet be alone with God, and that somehow, in ways not yet clearly defined, this was to be my lot.[1]

During the next ten years I went through the usual process of education, at first at home, in two day-schools run respectively by the daughter of a Protestant clergyman and two Anglican ladies. This was good ecumenical experience and raised the whole puzzling question of the divisions among Christians, to which no one seemed to have any very satisfactory answer. I then went as a boarder for five years to the Convent of the Sacred Heart at Hove.

Throughout this time the sense of inner alienation grew steadily stronger, though externally I got on quite well with my contemporaries and led an outwardly fairly normal life except for periodic bouts of opting out.[2] The sense of the inner unity of all things and the desire to discover how they were related to each other in their ultimate cause became practically an obsession; these lines from Francis Thompson's "Mistress of Vision" haunted me for months:

> All things hiddenly
> to each other linkéd are,
> so that thou canst not stir a stone
> without troubling of a star.[3]

For a time I was keenly interested in alchemy, but only theoretically. The sense of living in two dimensions became almost habitual at this stage. I had a passionate desire for intellectual coherence, and the elementary philosophy classes that formed a normal part of our curriculum were immensely helpful in sorting out my categories at the level of rational thought. Christian doctrine classes I am afraid I found frankly boring for the most part, though there was a certain intellectual satisfaction in seeing how everything fitted so neatly together with an almost Cartesian clarity and distinctness of ideas. There was however at the same time a perpetual need to "go beyond," a recognition that there was a whole other way of knowing, or at least that not everything could be grasped by the thinking mind: once again, the grid did not fit the whole of the experience. However, fortunately for me and my contemporaries, our spiritual formation as a whole was in wise and holy hands. We had a very sound and practical training in self-discipline, nicely geared to our capacities and needs. The Eucharist was at the heart of our life, and we were taught very practically and unsentimentally to enter into this making-present of the life-giving death of the Lord, who became a real and living influence. We learned Gregorian chant and I loved it: there was plenty of depth and mystery there, but I must confess that I did not get any explicit help with my basic quest, the effort somehow to get into immediate touch with the Mystery beyond all names and forms, which yet felt so bafflingly near. The world of official Christianity seemed to be a solid, this-worldly universe, and the world to come was not, it seemed, so very different. The only attempt I ever made to get some enlightenment met with such a snub that I never repeated the direct approach: I said tentatively to one of the nuns, having, I suppose, found some reference in a book, "There is none of St. John of the Cross in the (school) library, is there?" I don't remember exactly what she said, but I realized all too well that I had asked something considered most improper for a sixteen-year-old.

The storm-center was not yet, as it later became, the person of Jesus. The very sane formation regarding the Eucharist we received at school made a deep impression: a sense of the living dynamism of the presence and action of Christ in the world of today and of the centrality of the cross as the *axis mundi*, like the cosmic pillar or tree of Indian tradition[4] on which all life depends, certainly opened out into mystery, and was a steady point of reference in dark times, of which there were many. I think it was also this habit of entering into the movement of the return of the Lord to the Father in his life-giving death which gave me a strong sense of his being in truth the Way, as he himself said, and not, in his human nature at least, the End. This, however, was not yet explicit.

One further lesson I learnt painfully from experience before leaving school, which was essential to Christian spirituality as well as to all three main schools of Vedānta: however desperately one may seek to know "That from which speech turns back, together with the mind, being unable to reach it," this is not possible unless "the Self reveals itself," or as Jesus said, "it is made known by the Son." Similarly one cannot be freed from the blocks of selfish attachments or ambition unless the grave is given and the spring touched from within: all one can do is to strive as best one may and "pray for this consummation to the exclusion of all else," as I later discovered Śaṅkara put it.

I left school in the summer of 1940 and went home for a year. In the following September, I entered the noviceship of the Society of the Sacred Heart, evacuated to the beauty and austerity of an empty half of Kinross House on Loch Leven.

As far as my overall quest went, I was by this time almost at the end of my tether. The focus was now on the apparent dichotomy between the world of everyday experience, including the ordinary goals of human living, and what is known in India as the *Paramapuruṣārtha*, the supreme goal of human existence. The situation was not improved by the well-meant lamentations of friends who deplored my decision to "shut myself off from the world" when, they kindly insisted, I was eminently fitted to do it so much good with all my manifold gifts and endowments. The problem, as always, was one of relation: how to make the breakthrough, find the door into the secret garden, reconcile the apparently conflicting claims of the temporal and eternal. A year or two later my Mistress of Novices, Margaret Shepherd, read us a poem by her brother Eric, of "Murder in a Nunnery" fame, which would certainly have made complete sense to me at that moment in the light of my earlier experiences and brought some measure of peace. It was called "The Return of Innocence ." I quote from memory but I think fairly accurately:

> In a feeling numbness,
> a hearing deafness and a seeing blindness,
> she cometh swiftly where all loving-kindness
> greeteth with words of dumbness
> her in the garden with the river flowing.
>
> No man its secret wists,
> it openeth when it lists,
> that inner door,
> yielding firm foothold where there is no floor:
> some power that is not she
> turneth the key
> upon that blissful, free,
> effortless, unutterable outgoing
> into the garden with the river flowing.

In the meantime, as soon as I had picked up Margaret Shepherd's first letter to me in the hall at home, I knew even without opening it that I had at last found someone who knew what I was seeking.[5]

"The Appearance of Duality"

It is not possible to speak of non-duality unless there is at least the appearance of duality. (Śaṅkarācārya)

That intuition proved correct, but the noviceship and the years that followed it were nearly the end of me. The unacknowledged non-dualist was confronted squarely by the at least apparent theological and spiritual dualism of the pre-Vatican Catholic Church, a dualism whose origins, I gradually came to realize, reached right back to the early centuries of Christianity and the curvature of the spine introduced not only into theology but also into the liturgical and spiritual life of the Church by the great Christological heresies—especially the Arian heresy, for if it is true that worship provides the norm for belief, the reverse can be equally true. The effects of the reaction against the denial of the divinity of Christ by Arius and his followers can quickly be grasped by comparing the pre- and post-Arian formulations of the very ancient shorter Christian doxology. In its present form the first part runs: "glory be to the Father *and* the Son *and* the Holy Spirit." The pre-Arian formula was "Glory be to the Father *through* the Son *in* the Holy Spirit": in other words, it clearly evoked the dynamism of the Word "coming forth from the Father" and "returning to the Father," making it quite plain that the Father, the mysterious Source without a Source, and not the Son, was ultimately the Origin and End of all things, and that the Christian life was a sharing, in and through the Spirit, in the life of the Son—a life wholly *a Patre* and *ad Patrem*. Faced by denial of the divinity of the Lord, the natural reaction of the Church was to stress it vigorously, and the long-term consequence was that Christ was no longer seen so much as the First-born among many brethren and our mediator with the Father, but rather as the divine King throned in glory, only too easily tending to take first place in the worship and devotion of the Christian people. The result of this failure to remember the true role of the humanity of

Christ as "a guiding hand leading us to the Godhead," which is, as St. Thomas Aquinas puts it, "the proper object of devotion," was a gradual loss of awareness of the dynamic orientation of Christian life of which the early Church had been so deeply conscious, and corresponding tendency to equate the following of Christ with a *dualistic imitation from without* rather than *an entry into his very life and consciousness of being "from"* *and "to" the Father.* The mystics were for the most part honourable exceptions to this tendency, but they gradually came to be regarded as a race apart, whose lot one could not hope to emulate without serious danger to one's humility.[6]

So the sense of mystery was gradually drained out of Christianity, which was largely reduced to virtuous behaviour and a loving devotion to the person of Jesus. Luckily for me and my contemporaries, my Mistress of Novices was herself a mystic, but did not hold at all with the "race apart" theory, at least not in the usually accepted sense. She was a deeply contemplative woman with a keen sense of humor and a mind of her own, and by the time I met her, her fundamental purpose in life was to help her novices along the road of contemplative prayer. She was still thinking out her theological position on this, and the synthesis worked out by the great Dominican, Reginald Garrigou-Lagrange, between the teaching of St. Thomas Aquinas on the normal development of the life of grace and that of the great mystics on the ways of prayer was a great source of inspiration to her. She was convinced that a profound "experience of God," as the expression goes today, was the birthright of every Christian, the normal outcome of the steady growth in love to which we are all called by the Gospel. She shared her insights with us both privately and in unforgettable classes on Christian theology, though the teaching on Christology, the Church, and the sacraments was largely post-Tridentine—Vatican II was still twenty years in the future— and the revolutionary developments taking place in scripture studies and theology on the continent were largely unknown to us because of the war. She greatly helped me in my search for unity in my own life by her solidly theological teaching on grace, "the seed of glory—a certain beginning of eternal life" here and now, and on fidelity to the inner prompting of the Spirit as basically the expression of the same inner attitude at prayer and throughout the day.

At that time the English province of the Society of the Sacred Heart[7] was strongly influenced by the prevailing fear in the Catholic Church of mysticism, which was most emphatically thought not to be for the young, who needed to learn self-discipline, obedience, and a proper humility. No one would quarrel with the positive side of this programme, but as Mistress of Novices, Margaret Shepherd had to walk on the Upanishadic razor's edge as she sought to betray neither her own deep inner convictions nor her responsibility to "form" us according to the Spirit and traditions of our Society. The situation was made more difficult by the fact that we were almost completely cut off by the war from the Mother House in Rome, so there was no court of appeal, though the Mistress of Novices was at that time directly responsible to the Mother General for all that concerned her office. I did not of course realize all this then, though we novices did fairly soon become aware that a question mark hung over the way in which we were being "formed."

One of my first problems in the noviceship, which could well have been fatal as far as my future in the Society was concerned, was the early-nineteenth-century theology and spirituality of our Constitutions. Basically, as I later came to realize after much determinedly honest study of the writings and spirit of our foundress and her times, there was practically nothing there which could not be reconciled with the most authentic Christian tradition if one made due allowance for sociocultural factors—in fact there was in the Constitutions a deeply contemplative and unifying spirit fully in harmony with the most radical non-dualism. This however did not at once leap to the eye of a candidate whose convictions at that time were neatly summed up in the words of the Imitation of Christ: "He to whom all things are one and who sees all things in one and draws all things to one *potest stabilis esse corde et in Deo pacificus permanere."* (The last clause defies translation.)[8] "This little Society," said the Constitutions firmly, "is wholly consecrated to the glory of the Sacred Heart of Jesus and to the propagation of its worship. Such is the end which all those who become members must propose to themselves." This it seemed to me I could never do: how could anything be the *end* of my life but the immense and unfathomable Mystery who was not only my Beginning and End, the Source without a Source, but also the Origin and End of Jesus himself as Word made flesh? This was of course not a new problem, but the old one suddenly become impossibly concrete and acute. At last I decided that I had to settle this once and for all, even if it meant my having to leave the Society. I went to Margaret Shepherd and after due preliminaries cautiously enquired: "Mother, the incarnation is a *means*, isn't it?" I shall never forget the spontaneous joy with which she quickly turned to me and said: "*Yes*, my dearie, that's *exactly it!*" This was to me a tremendous relief, but she was not the whole Society, let alone the whole Church, and for years I was beset by the recurrent temptation to go off and become a Trappist, a hermit, anything but a member of a Society which expressed its end in such, to me, unsatisfactory terms. I was still torn apart by, on the one hand, the passion for intellectual clarity and synthesis and, on the other, the obsessive conviction that no intellectual statement could fully express the ultimate Truth which necessarily was to the human mind either a great darkness or inaccessible light, both of which seemed to come in the end to the same thing. All this was of course compounded by the fact that it was not a mere theory but my life-commitment that was at stake.

It was impossible to forget this dilemma, because it was forced on my attention every evening when we had to prepare for our morning meditation. We were supposed to write "points" based on a Gospel ingredient, according to what was then generally regarded as *the* "Ignatian method" of meditating, whereas in reality many of us never used the points at all:

we were nearly all drawn to a silent way of prayer without many, or even at times any, words. Yet this could not be publicly acknowledged because in the Society, or at least in the English Province at that time, novices were officially supposed to meditate with mind and imagination on the life of Jesus. This disturbed me greatly, for even though Margaret Shepherd explained to us that though it was good to follow the normal pattern of preparation for the sake of our education, there was no obligation to use the points at the time of prayer, the mere fact of having to compose them, not to mention the necessity of not letting other members of the Society know that we were really praying as we did, revolted my instinct for openness and integrity: why could we not simply be ourselves and follow the path we were drawn to without fear? Maybe I was too absolute at this time, but I was not happy over the apparently double path, though there was, it seemed, no way out of the dilemma just then.

It had already been decided that if I survived the noviceship I should go to Oxford (if they would have me!) and read Greats, so I again took up Greek, of which I had done a little at school, and was also turned loose on the *Summa Theologica* of St. Thomas. I went through it from beginning to end, objections first, trying to answer them all, then St. Thomas's solutions, then the body of the text. It was an extraordinarily satisfying experience, only equaled years later by reading the *Divina Commedia* of Dante in the original, and still later the commentary of Śaṅkarācārya on the Brahmasūtras. The *Summa Theologica* may not be everyone's idea of the perfect handbook of non-dualist theology, but even then I dimly apprehended the non-dual intuition underlying the immense and orderly detail of Thomas's exposition of Christian theology. Some things I found oddly disappointing: his theology of the Trinity in terms of relation is the key to whatever understanding is possible to our bat-like minds of that blazing darkness. His attempts to explain the mode of being and function of the "separated soul" after death left me with more questions than answers about the metaphysical possibility of individual survival of death, a subject about which, interestingly enough, I later found Śaṅkara equally ambiguous, and his treatment of the fate of babies who died without baptism struck me as an extraordinary let-down: on Thomas's own wise and comprehensive principles there must, I felt, be a better solution than that. At about the same time I came upon his apophatic theology in the commentaries on the Pseudo-Denys, and the Questing Beast, still very much alive, fell upon them ravenously: *"in fine nostrae cognitionis, Deum tamquam ignotum congnoscimus—Deo tamquam omnino ignoto conjungimur."*[9] This was better even than St. John of the Cross, whose *Ascent of Mount Carmel* especially had been a revelation a year or two earlier. Jacques Maritain's *Degrés du Savoir* also contributed immensely to a process of clarifying fields of knowledge and ways of knowing which was necessarily ongoing.

I duly got into Oxford and read Greats at St. Anne's. It was a marvelous though tough experience. My college generously allowed me to have the tutorials (with the Dominicans of Blackfriars) for a special paper on St. Thomas to bridge the gulf between Plato and Descartes, but refused to sanction the writing of a paper for schools: Greats, they said, was enough for any woman without extras.

During my four years at Oxford I was really fighting a war on two fronts. There was first of all the tremendous challenge of the academic side of life—the reading of endless classical texts and doing of countless Greek and Latin proses during the first five terms, and later the writing of regular essays on such preposterous subjects as "Time, Space, and Matter as the Principle of Individuation" (all one subject) specially devised by my philosophy tutor in my final year, Miss Iris Murdoch, as she then was, for a self-opinionated Thomist too prone to quotation and facile generalization. I found it very difficult to take the Oxford philosophy of that time seriously—there seemed to be an almost universal fear of confronting really crucial issues or ultimate questions. Sir David Ross's famous parcel containing a borrowed book which got lost in the post seems in retrospect to have occupied weeks of earnest reflection at lectures on the degree of responsibility weighing on the borrower who had posted it back to the owner. I felt this problem could have been settled in less than five minutes by enquiring into the degree of care with which the parcel had been packed and posted. Both Professor Gilbert Ryle on Mrs. Beaton[10] as a model of linguistic usage and lectures on "Logical Positivism" I found frustrating to a degree: I could not understand how so many intelligent people could take the latter seriously when its first premise was so blatantly self-contradictory, as Ayer himself later admitted. I am still unable to explain all this rationally except as an expression of general loss of a sense of direction resulting from the war. That in fact seemed to be the problem: no one showed any signs of awareness of the existence of the other dimension of being, with very few exceptions. People even professed not to be sure if they could trust their senses because they saw the moon looking about the size of a half-crown, or a straight stick looking bent as it stood in water. Metaphysics was definitely out, though it soon began creeping back from the continent in the strange guise of existentialism, and a little later reappeared as a respectable citizen through the back door of the philosophy of religion. My philosophy tutors, thank God, took metaphysics seriously, though they gave me no quarter, and meetings with Iris Murdoch especially were for me real adventures of the mind.

From the point of view of non-dualism, apart from this interaction with gifted minds and the relentless formation to objective listening and reflection, perhaps the most valuable part of Oxford was the rigorous intellectual discipline of Latin and Greek prose composition. I realized in later years why Greats had been the supreme training-ground for the administrators of Empire: the weekly struggle to rethink a passage from Macaulay or a *Times* leader in terms of the mental processes of Cicero or Demosthenes was to prove an invaluable preparation for entering into the mind-set and worldview of a still more different culture. After leaving Oxford I read in a classical journal an article on translation called "Intermediate Thinking" which threw further light on this process; the author quoted St. Augustine: *"cogitamus enim omne quod dicimus illo interiori verbo quod ad nullius gentis pertinet linguam"* — "we think everything we say in that inner word which belongs to the language of no race of men." This glimpse of the possibility of catching meaning and holding it for a flying moment stripped of all human verbal expression, in a flash of intuition as it were, awakened a very deep echo.

The real action of the Oxford years took place on the other front, however, that of my basic life-commitment in relation to the dualistic presentation of Christianity prevalent at the time. In 1948, during the visit of our then Mother General to England, I attempted to clarify things with her: Margaret Shepherd had died as superior of our house at Oxford the year before, having been removed from the office of Mistress of Novices because her teaching on contemplative prayer as normal was at that time considered not orthodox, or anyway not suitable for young members of our Society. This had been disconcerting, to put it mildly, as it reopened for me the whole question of whether or not I could remain in the Society. The position had become more complicated by the fact that the Mother General of that time had been the superior of a Spanish co-adjutrix sister who had been subject to what she believed were visions of Jesus giving a "message" of love and mercy in terms which aroused in me the strongest negative reactions. After much hesitation and heart-searching, Mother de Lescure had decided that she could no longer doubt the genuineness of these visions, and when she became Mother General she propagated their teaching with such vigor that one might well have been forgiven for concluding that she believed the Society had been founded over a hundred and fifty years before solely with a view to communicating it. The focus was very much on the love, mercy, and suffering of Jesus and his desire for love and consolation in return, and this latter point I am afraid revolted me. Later on I was compelled to recognize that in spite of the uncongenial "names and forms" in which it was expressed, belonging to the visionary's own sociocultural and religious background, the essence of the teaching was fully in conformity with the Gospel, and its transforming action on people I knew and loved left no doubt possible as to the action of the Spirit through it, but its forms of expression were totally alien to me, and raised the old problem of the apparent absolutizing of Jesus as object of devotion in a way that seemed to underplay the mystery of the Godhead in its ultimate transcendence. I was probably not too tactful in my presentation of my difficulties, and I discovered only years later that Mother de Lescure had herself at that time been suffering agonies of doubt lest she had misled the whole Society by supporting the "Message." Anyway, I got short shrift. She told me to "forget all my Mistress of Novices had taught me, and trust the spirituality of the Society." This provoked such a crisis of integrity that I did not know where to turn: I had remained in the Society on the basis of my conviction that what my Mistress of Novices had taught me was in fact its genuine spirituality, and if it was not, then I could not see how I could continue to remain in it. On the other hand, I was halfway through Oxford, and it hardly seemed the moment to make a drastic life-decision. I decided to wait two years and come to a decision later. In this I was tacitly supported by my English superiors, for whose trust I can never be grateful enough. I took as my motto "He who is faithful in small things will be faithful also in greater," and lived it with an almost fanatic thoroughness. (The implicit non-dualism of this solution I realized only much later!)

At the end of the two years I knew I had to go ahead. Whatever the outward circumstances of my life, it would make no fundamental difference: the Eternal underpinned and permeated everything, and that was enough. I should in fairness add that I was in other ways very happy in my religious life: there was much mutual love and acceptance, and some, especially among my contemporaries, shared my deepest concerns. I have never regretted the decision to remain.

Looking back from the further shore, so to speak, this whole incident seems to me to highlight the fact that non-dualism is not merely a matter of intellectual conviction: it consists also in an existential experience, confirming intellectual conviction of the absolute transcendence-in-immanence of the ultimate Mystery in relation to all that exists or occurs at the relatively ephemeral level of "ordinary" life, a kind of wordless and con- ceptless adherence to the truth of one's own being which, how- ever obscure and painful, is also strangely liberating.

During the next six years, I worked in my own old school, teaching, then also in charge of the studies, and finally as head- mistress. At the same time I did a five-year theology course, mostly in the holidays. Though the theology textbook was pre- Vatican Tanquerey, in Latin, my theology tutor, the late Father Cedric Hardwick, was a man of genius and of God, and the scripture course was a marvelous initiation into modern bibli- cal studies. I verified in those years the truth of a remark Father Hardwick once made to me, the secret I am sure of his own depth of insight into "divine things": "There are two ways of knowing God—theological study and contemplative prayer, and *the more we give ourselves to theological study, the more God gives himself in contemplative prayer.*" Śaṅkara could hardly have put it better.

I was very happy during those years. I loved the children, especially the troublesome ones, and understood how their funny minds worked. The intellectual problem of dualism slipped into temporary abeyance, and the emphasis was more on the practical problem of transforming the cat that walked by itself into a joyful mother of kittens, to adapt a phrase from the Psalms, coping with the day-to-day details of school-life.

However, the Questing Beast was by no means dead. Perhaps a certain acosmism remained: anyway, I began to feel that I was too comfortably dug in and too much involved in "this world." The old pull to the desert, the mountain, the "beyond all name and form" at last became so strong that I responded to an appeal for volunteers for Brazil, where our Society had been for some hundred years. I knew nothing of Brazil and had no desire to go there, only a blind sense that I had to obey the inner impulsion to this apparently crazy initiative. When the answer came, "Not Brazil, but India," my interior reaction was so violent and so overwhelmingly negative that it surprised even myself. It felt like a death sentence (though I knew practically nothing of India either!), but I knew I had to go through with it, and what was more, put a good face on it, for the news could not be made public until the end of the school year, three months away: that school had had six headmistresses in ten years and neither girls nor parents were in a mood to welcome another change. I was faced once more with both clear perception and the gut-level experience of the tension between the Eternal and the passing, and also by the recognition of the impossibility of resolving the dilemma by cutting off one of its horns. In theory I was free to go or not to go—representation of difficulties was always possible—but whether I went or not, the problem of reconciling the unchanging and the ephemeral would remain: the terms in which it was expressed would make no difference. In practice I knew I had to go: I could not have lived with my own refusal.

It really was a death, and the preliminary to a rebirth, though I could not guess that then. I arrived in India in October 1956, never, as I supposed, to return, for until Vatican II this was the normal practice. It soon became evident to me that nothing I had ever learnt was of any relevance any more (so at least it seemed). I was to be Head of the Philosophy Department in Sophia College for Women, a constituent college of Bombay University, but the academic year began only in June, so I began to study Hindi and Indian Philosophy and was in charge of the general order and discipline of the college.

I was still pretty dualistic at least as far as Christianity and other religions were concerned, and to my shame I tore up month after month, with barely a glance, the first issues of the "Mountain Path," the journal of the Sri Ramanashram at Tiruvannamalai, Tamil Nadu, where the greatest advaitin of modern times had died five years earlier. However, my horizons were soon widened.

The staff and students of Sophia College were drawn from all religious communities. As I came to know and love them, it became quite clear that in spite of all our differences the same Spirit was at work in all of us. Philosophy in all its branches was a marvelous meeting-ground for minds, but very soon a new and very searching question presented itself: what exactly was I, as a Christian educator, supposed to be doing for my students, who were mostly not Christians? I realized that if I thought I was meant to get them all baptized into the Christian fold, I might as well pack up and go home at once. Conversion in that sense hardly ever happened, and with good reason: girls depended wholly on their families to arrange their marriage. Any girl who changed her religion would ipso facto be on her own (mixed marriages were far rarer in those days than they are now, and even today they can pose serious problems). To "preach the Gospel" in such a way as to create a false conscience in my students, making them feel they had a moral obligation to do something which was in fact morally impossible for them, was clearly not on. I came to the conclusion that my role was, as St. Ignatius says in his directives to retreat-givers, to seek to establish and foster that relationship between the creature and Creator which would allow the Creator to deal freely with his creatures. This I understood to mean helping them to form themselves to an integrity of mind and heart which would lead them to acknowledge truth wherever they met it, and follow it out to the end.

This whole question of missionary activity was much discussed in India at the time, and a few years later I became
directly involved in theological reflection on the subject when
I was invited as an observer to the seminar on Christianity and
World Religions held in Bombay in December 1964, in connection with the Eucharistic Congress, and attended by Hans
Küng and other theological luminaries. Questions were raised
here which now look very elementary, but at that time were
quite bold, such as: Was it part of our task as Christian educators to help Hindus to be better Hindus? Might we allow them
to perform their own worship in our hostels? Or encourage
. and even help them to study their own scriptures? Were followers of other faiths saved because or in spite of their own
religions?

From then on I was in the thick of theological reflection,
involved at both regional and national levels in the All India
Seminar on the Church in India Today in 1969, a member of the
Commissio Technica for the renewal of seminary formation
and engaged in courses for the renewal of religious life for
women, and taking part in the regional and international Conferences on the Theology of Evangelization (Nagpur, 1971) and
the follow-up Pastoral Conference on Evangelization in Patna
in 1974, as well as the Monastic Conference in Bangalore in
1974. At the latter, a major issue became the apparent dualism
of the attitude of the contemplative orders, segregating themselves from the Church and the world at large, whereas there
was such openly expressed need of help and guidance in prayer
for Christians throughout the country.

In 1975 I represented Sophia College at an international
meeting in Delhi of Catholic universities and theological faculties, at which some of us got a resolution passed recognizing
as a top priority the attempt to re-express our Christian faith
in the redemptive incarnation of the Word of God in terms that
make sense to modern man in all the pluriformity of his sociocultural situation. I do not know if this has had any effect.

My own Society was one of the pioneers in India after Vatican II in what is now known as "inculturation" and in 1972 we reopened the CPS Ashram, Pune, as an ecumenical venture in collaboration with the Community of St. Mary the Virgin of Wantage, who had been in India for nearly a hundred years, through the good offices of Bishop Christopher Robinson, chairman of the board of trustees, who remained our true and wise guide and friend until his death in 1988. I was one of those who volunteered for this. It seemed to be directly in line with the ancient longings of the Questing Beast.

When I arrived in India, I had begun to face the challenge of integrating my double heritage as a Scot and an Indian by adoption without being unfaithful to either, for as I have already said, I did not expect ever to return to Great Britain. In Pune, as an ecumenical community, we had first of all to transcend the differences between our Church backgrounds, Anglican, Roman Catholic, and later Evangelical, by finding our common identity as Christians in the Gospel we all shared, and also, "in our daily contact with our brothers and sisters of other religions, constantly to recognize in their religious experience the striking resonances of the same ineffable Mystery which Jesus Christ revealed to us as beyond all adequate expression" (from the statement of the seminar on Non-Biblical Scriptures held at the National Biblical, Catechetical, and Liturgical Centre in Bangalore in 1974). One or two examples of these "striking resonances" may be helpful. One of the pilgrim devotees of the poet saints of Maharashtra who are constantly in and out of the ashram, an old peasant, asked us once after the Eucharist, at which he had been present, what was the meaning of communion. We explained to him that God came to us in that form of food (a symbol familiar in his own tradition also). "But," he said with a wicked twinkle, "why bother with that? God is in *everything!*" The obvious answer, as he knew well, was "Then why do *you* go from place to place on pilgrimage?" Again, our old Panditji who spent a month with us in the early days in Pune, having read my doctoral thesis, agreed with me that belief in survival of the individual self was not incompatible with Śaṅkara's basic principles, though his actual position is not clear. "But," he said, shining eyes wide open in astonishment at such incomprehensible self-importance, "Why should one *want* to survive, once one realizes *he is all?*" Finally, an old and holy monk affiliated with the Ramakrishna Order stayed with us for about ten days just before Easter this year. He was shown the chapel, where the Sacrament is reserved. Next day he was up at four, sitting there motionless for about two hours. Later, when he was introduced to me, he said slowly and with great respect: "I must congratulate you on the atmosphere in your chapel. There is in this place a tremendous Presence—an immense Sanctity. I have visited many ashrams, but *nowhere else* have I found what I find here." "Deep calleth on deep," and what becomes of outward differences? They are simply transcended, and yet we each remained what we were—Hindu and Christian. This is really non-dualism in action at the level of ordinary life, though we did not think of it in those terms at the beginning. Such experiences have had, and still have, an influence on our whole way of thinking and being as a community. They form an extremely important part of the "alternative experience" of my title, and I shall return to them in my final lecture.

At the beginning of this lecture I quoted a phrase from George Gispert-Sauch, S.J.: "a quest that searches even for its own formulation." Perhaps I may conclude by summing up what were, I think, the findings of the Questing Beast on the threshold of its face-to-face encounter with the non-dualism of the Upanishads in its most radical form:

1. The whole of existence is underpinned and permeated by a fundamental unity.
2. This unity is apprehended/realized not by eliminating differences, but by transcending them.

3. It is not only perceived by the intelligence, but recognized by a gut-level instinct, expressed in a sense of desolation at its apparent absence (or one's absence from it) and a joy and repose in its presence in which one's whole being is brought at least temporarily into harmony with all that is or ever can be.

Notes

1. Something that has always intrigued me about this experience is the appalling sense of desolation I suffered at the total absence of boys. I think that even at the age of eight it had something to do with an obscure intuition that one cannot simply wipe out half of reality at the level of "pairs of opposites." Both have to be reckoned with, or an essential balance is disturbed.

2. Usually facilitated by minor mishaps such as being providentially hit on the head by a cricket ball, the effects of which I did not underestimate. That cricket ball earned me almost a whole summer term of peaceful reflection.

3. Another powerful influence dating from this period which affected my whole life was a Latin chant from the liturgy for the festival of St. Madeleine Sophie Barat, foundress of the Society of the Sacred Heart: "I sought for wisdom openly in my prayer: from my youth up I sought after her. . . . To him who gives me wisdom I will give glory." It was a constant life-line in times of darkness and storm.

4. This pillar "holds even opposites together, it is a tree whose branches are Being and Non-being. . . . all values that men acknowledge as authentic are rooted in it"; "The one on whom the Lord of life leant for support when he propped up the world—Tell me of that Support—who may he be?" (see Artharva Veda 10. 7 and the commentary by Raimundo Panikkar, *The Vedic Experience* [Berkeley: University of California Press, 1977], pp. 61, 63). The image clearly points beyond itself to the ultimate Ground and Support.

5. I cannot remember exactly what she said in that first letter but I know the assurance was there that single-hearted search for God could in the end only be of benefit to "*His*" world." Some thirty years

later the old cousin of Ramana Maharshi assured me that "the silence of the man of understanding (the contemplative or *jñāni*) is not a dead silence—it is a perpetual *tapas* (meritorious act of self-discipline) of benefit to the entire world."

6. The aberrations of the Illuminati and later the Quietists, among others, and also Luther's teaching on grace as the cloak of Christ's merits thrown over our sins, made ecclesiastical authorities wary and contributed to the obscuring of awareness of the transforming and vitally renewing power of grace and its strong thrust of "return to the Source" as a springing fountain *within* each believer.

7. A religious society of contemplative educators founded in France in 1800. Its fundamental inspiration is and has always been union and conformity with the mind and heart of Christ. Its practical task has always been envisaged in the perspective of eternity, as the renewal of society by the education of girls to be women of faith and of intelligent and selfless service.

8. Nevertheless one should probably attempt it: "is able to be steadfast of heart and abide peacefully in God."

9. "At the end of our knowing we know God as unknown: we are united to God as to something wholly unknown."

10. Author of a famous cookery book.

The Challenge of Advaita

I first met the challenge of advaita or non-dualism in the Hindu tradition in 1957, soon after my arrival in India and some fifteen years before we reopened the C.P.S. Ashram in Pune, through the books prescribed by the University of Bombay for the B.A. course in Indian Philosophy which I had to teach. It was an exhilarating but baffling experience. Both I and my students found Śaṅkara's thought as there presented thoroughly mystifying, but it was clear that there was here some very profound and exciting intuition. This was most frustrating, and when a few years later I was asked to work for a doctorate in any field of Indian philosophy I chose, I knew at once what I must do: learn Sanskrit, go back to the original texts, and find out what Śaṅkara was really saying. At about the same time I met Dom Henri LeSaux, O.S.B., known in India as Swami Abhishiktananda, and translated his book *Rencontre de l'Hindouisme et du Christianisme*, though it was a review of his later book, *Sagesse Hindoue, Mystique Chrétienne*, that originally drew me to him. This encounter was epoch-making for me.

Abhishiktanandaji together with Father Jules Monchanin had founded Shantivanam Ashram in Tamilnadu, later taken over by Father Bede Griffiths, in 1948. He had visited the Sri Ramanashram at Tiruvannamalai before the death of Sri Ramana Maharshi and had there been completely overwhelmed by an experience of ultimate reality which seemed to relativize everything—all "names and forms," in the traditional Hindu phrase, all images and concepts, all myths and symbols. Under the impact of this boundless ocean of Being, he was compelled to ask himself what became of the individual and his pitifully limited being, the claims of Christianity, the uniqueness of Christ as way of salvation, the Church and all her teachings. Swamiji (Abhishiktananda) was a Benedictine monk, he had staked his whole life on his faith in Christ, and in his sober moments he could not doubt that faith, but neither could he see how to reconcile it with the truth of this other experience which to him was self-authenticating. I did not however realize until much later, and especially after his death, when I read the almost indecipherable manuscript of his journal, the anguish which he had gone through, and to which he was still subject at intervals. When I first met him he was still wrestling with the whole experience as a theological problem at the level of the thinking mind. In the depths he knew that truth cannot contradict truth, and was convinced of the validity of both advaita and Christian revelation. He had attempted to work out a synthesis in *Sagesse* which helped many people, though to his distress it was regarded as dangerous by some Christian theologians whom he both loved and respected. He later declared that he had gone far beyond it, and toward the end of his life could hardly be brought to give his attention to revising the text for a new edition of the English translation. What helped me most about *Sagesse* was not so much the attempted theological synthesis as the extraordinarily lucid presentation of Ramana Maharshi and his Upanishadic experience, and Abhishiktananda's encounter with it at Tiruvannamalai, though his likening of the experience of the *rishis** to the "awakening" of the human consciousness of Christ at the moment of his resurrection had

---

* The original seers of Vedic truth.

a very powerful impact on me and remained, I think, as a half-conscious point of reference as I fought for my own survival as a thinking Christian animal.

For in spite, or perhaps because, of all my involvement in Church renewal and theological reflection, this encounter with non-dualism through the person of Swamiji hit me like a bomb. What had struck me as alien and somehow repulsive when Ramana Maharshi first appeared upon my desk I now recognized as insidiously and dangerously connatural, rousing all the old craving for an absolute and ultimate unity which would justify the relativising of all conceptualizations. I could not see how to argue with this enemy within the gates, so large a part of me insistently affirmed its truth.

All my ancient questionings reawakened: the apparent preoccupation of Christianity with "names and forms" and this world, the suspicion of the apophatic way of prayer, then still largely prevalent in the Church, the increasingly obvious inadequacy of the traditional presentation of Christ as the only way to salvation, the intolerable caricature of God the Father implicit in the "satisfaction" theory of redemption, not yet officially repudiated: and the accompanying near-absolutizing of the deified humanity of Christ, which so often seemed, at least in practice, to make the incarnation an end in itself. All this was further complicated for me by some of the effects on my own Congregation of the renewal of religious life launched by Vatican II, in particular the giving up of cloister and all that was considered "monastic" in favor of a more outgoing , secular, and active way of life, all of which seemed to go directly counter to the inborn drive of the Questing Beast toward the desert and "knowledge of things in their ultimate causes," the Mystery beyond all name and form and the stability of a basically contemplative way of life. I was in fact still subject to bouts of acosmism which I had not yet learnt to recognize as more dualist than non-dualist in character. I had the feeling of being on the verge of some tremendous discovery, full of risk and danger—literally *tremendum et fascinans,* exhilarating and yet obscurely terrifying.

It was in this somewhat turbulent state of mind that I began my serious study of advaita in the light of the commentaries of Śaṅkarācārya.

CLEARING THE GROUND

As I had not the faintest idea of what had and had not been done by way of research in this field, I consulted Dr. R. V. De Smet, S. J., of De Nobili College, Pune, recognized throughout India as an authority on the different schools of Indian philosophy and especially on Advaita Vedānta. He had done his own doctoral research on "The Theological Method of Śaṅkara." He advised me to explore Śaṅkara's concept of relation, saying that this was a subject he had hoped to explore further himself, but he did not think he would now have time to do so. He gave me a few other helpful suggestions, including that of reading A. Krempel's exhaustive study on relation in St. Thomas Aquinas,[1] as he thought the fundamental intuition of Śaṅkara on relation was strikingly similar to that of St. Thomas. He added that the crucial term for understanding Śaṅkara's own peculiar concept of relation was *tādātmya*—literally, "having 'That' as one's self." I emerged from the encounter feeling like a minnow floundering in the Atlantic, but I had found a steadfast friend whose comments were invaluable to me in the years that followed.

One more invaluable piece of advice was given to me by that wise and holy man, the late Father Julian Bayart, S. J., then rector of the Pontifical Athenaeum in Pune (now known as Jnana Deepa Vidyapeeth), who told me never to forget that Śaṅkara was primarily teaching not a philosophy of being, but a way of salvation through knowledge.

My first task was to learn enough Sanskrit to read the texts in the original. Fortunately the Sanskrit of Śaṅkara is rather like the Latin of St. Thomas, business-like and extremely consistent in the use of terms, with a reasonably limited vocabulary. The next step was to try to ascertain which of the relevant texts ascribed to Śaṅkara were in fact his, for owing to his eminence and the fact that the heads of the four *maths* or centers of teaching he established in India have all borne the title of Śaṅkarācārya from that day to this, a certain amount of false attribution has naturally taken place. In this area I had to rely a great deal on the consensus of scholars, though later, with growing experience, I dared to form an opinion of my own on one or two texts where opinion is divided, for example, the commentaries on the Māṇḍūkya Upanishad and Kārikā. The Māṇḍūkya texts were especially important, for they more than any others lend themselves to the "world-negating pessimist" interpretation of Śaṅkara and are in fact quoted almost to the exclusion of all others by supporters of this interpretation. (For the record, I came to the conclusion that their authenticity is extremely doubtful.)

This whole question of the authenticity of texts was crucially important for me because of the remarkable lack of agreement as to the genuine thought of Śaṅkara, which already existed a hundred years after his death. I fairly soon realized that, as I had suspected, when my students and I wrestled with the textbook Śaṅkara we were shadow-boxing. I realized too that, in addition to the reason already given, there had been four other contributing causes to the misunderstanding of Śaṅkara's teaching which may be summed up as follows:

1. The extreme radicality of his demands: the seeker's whole being has to be brought into harmony with his quest. Even today in India it is accepted that the paths of *bhakti* or loving devotion and *karma* or dedicated service are the normal ways for the vast majority of people, who are not for the most part troubled by the dualism of ordinary experience. The experience of the Eternal is habitually mediated to them through the sacrament of the cosmos, and they are content

that it should be so, without being tormented by the driving impulse to "go beyond." The *jñāna mārga* or path of knowledge often appears to them as a threat, and they therefore lack the sympathy essential to real understanding.

2. Like Plato before him, Śaṅkara was gravely hampered by a linguistic problem. While he agreed that the universe pre-existed in its cause in some way, and therefore adopted the term *satkāryavāda* currently in use to express this view, he totally disagreed with the Sāṃkhya doctrine of creation by real transformation or evolution of the cause, which unfortunately was habitually expressed by using the same generic term. He was concerned above all to maintain the absolute transcendence and "one-without-a second" character of the ultimate Reality, Brahman or the Ātman, the Supreme Self. Therefore he was obliged to insist so strongly that created being was not being in the absolute sense of the Being of Ātman-Brahman, that he was understood by some to be relegating created being to the realm of unreality or illusion in the sense in which we understand those terms today. That this was by no means his intention is clear from a passage in the *Brahmasūtrabhāṣya* (which has apparently attracted too little attention), in which he states that a thing is real insofar as it does not undergo change: therefore when he refers to the world of creation as "unreal," what he means is that it is subject to change. At the same time, because of our innate tendency to stop at the level of our ordinary experience, without piercing through to the ultimate Reality it both reveals and veils, he recognized that it had a certain illusory character. Metaphysically speaking, however, it had a definite status of its own as essentially relative, absolutely dependent being.

The term *māyā*, illusion or magic, beloved of later Vedāntins, is never used by Śaṅkara in the causal sense of "creating illusion" precisely because this term had been used by some Buddhists to express their view of the total unreality of mundane beings, a view which he himself explicitly rejected. Much damage was done by later commentators who freely used the term *māyā* to interpret Śaṅkara's teaching, which was even described by some as *māyāvāda*, or "the doctrine of *māyā*," as though illusion-creating magic were a central theme of his thought. This led to endless confusion and needless questioning about the origin of the "cosmic illusion" and the locus of the *avidyā* or ignorance which is the advaitic equivalent of original sin, the root of all evil.

3. The enthusiasm with which nineteenth-century Western idealists hailed Śaṅkara as a natural ally and blood-brother has largely determined the prevailing image of Śaṅkara, and indeed of Vedānta as a whole, among Hindu scholars who have been influenced by Western philosophical thought down to our own time—an image that spread from them even to the common man who had undergone no such direct influence. Now, however, there is a movement of return to the original texts which is opening up fascinating possibilities for better understanding of the great Vedāntins Śaṅkara, Rāmānuja, and Madhva, their relationship to each other, and their contemporary relevance.

4. Fourthly, and finally, perhaps one of the greatest single influences in the obscuring of Śaṅkara's real meaning is the traditional Hindu method of exegesis, which has consisted for centuries in commenting on the commentators without direct reference to the original text. One of my colleagues, a Madhva scholar, told me that in all his study of Madhva, the fourteenth-century founder of the so-called dualist school of Vedānta and a bitter opponent of Śaṅkara, he had not found a scrap of evidence to suggest that Madhva had actually read Śaṅkara's own commentaries. There is still a certain amount of reluctance to adopt the methods of textual criticism in conservative Hindu circles, analogous to that faced by biblical scholars in the West in the nineteenth century, but there is also a growing realization of the new life this

approach can awaken in old texts. The whole situation is really rather exciting, not least in the possibilities it opens for interfaith theological reflection at a very deep level.

The Upanishadic Background

Śaṅkara did not regard his teaching on salvation through knowledge as an absolutely original discovery: he presented it as an interpretation—in his eyes the only true interpretation—of the teaching of the seers of the Upanishads on the supreme goal of human existence. It is therefore necessary to say something about that teaching here.

It is well known that the most diverse interpretations have been put upon the Upanishads by later thinkers: all the six great systems of Indian philosophy claim descent from them, and on that basis they are known as the "orthodox" systems, as distinct from Buddhism, Jainism, and the Cārvāka school of gross materialism (said by some to have existed only as a hypothetical opponent in the imaginations of followers of other systems). In spite of this, there is certainly a very characteristic Upanishadic outlook on the world which is in marked contrast to that inherited by Western man from his Hebrew and Greek ancestors. In this tradition the universe is permeated by a supreme creative and sustaining Presence which is itself the sole ultimate Reality and is to be approached not by rising above the high places of the earth to some empyrean heaven, but rather by withdrawing into the depths of one's own being, which is both thoroughly rooted in the earth and yet ultimately also in the Eternal. According to Upanishadic tradition, realization takes place through a successive awakening of deeper and deeper levels of consciousness, from that of the physical body constituted by food (the *annamayakośa*), through the *prāṇamayakośa* or "self of life" or "breath" and sense perception, the *manomayakośa* or discursive mind and imaginative and affective powers, the *vijñāna-mayakośa* or simple intelligence or intuition, and finally the *ānandamayakośa* or "self of bliss," beyond which there is nothing but the supreme Self or Ātman, unless indeed the *ānandamayakośa* is itself the supreme Self, a point on which commentators are not agreed.

It is essential to understand that the *kośas* are not to be thought of literally as "layers" of the individual, as it were; they are rather progressively richer dimensions of the person. The body is a living sensate body in and through which the mind and imagination acquire their sustenance or "raw material" and the intelligence enters into communion with the outer world. The truly "realized" man is a fully integrated person responding to the rest of the cosmos, of which he is very much a part, from the inmost depths of his being, a response in which every dimension of that being is harmoniously activated. The whole ascetic enterprise of one who would "know Brahman" is directed to the establishment of this perfect harmony, so that the radiance of the supreme Self can shine out undimmed by any disturbance at the level of body, mind, or intelligence (spirit, as we would say). Realization, therefore, does not involve an abandonment of the world in any pessimistic or destructive sense, but rather is the discovery that the deepest Reality within oneself is the deepest Reality at the heart of all being. In fact, the supreme insight of the whole Upanishadic tradition is precisely this recognition, through experience and not merely as a matter of intellectual assent, that ultimately there is neither "within" nor "without," for the Ground of the extramental universe is also the Ground of the individual self. Yet the earth and all it contained, including individual human beings, were very much there for Upanishadic man, in all their concrete individuality: as Śaṅkara himself was to say later, "When I see a post, I see a post," by which he meant a solid, extramental post, not a mental image of one. The great questions therefore remained, to haunt generation after generation: "What

lies beyond life?" "Explain to me the mystery of Brahman!"—
"That from which speech turns back, together with the mind,
being unable to reach it. . . ." What was the inmost nature of
that supreme Reality? How could it be related to man and to
the rest of the cosmos, without prejudice to its utter transcendence? What did the Chāndogya Upanishad mean when it said
that it was "One only, without a second"? Above all, how did
one come to know it? These were the questions faced by
Śaṅkarācārya when he began his life's work of reestablishing
the theological foundations of Hinduism, which had suffered
serious erosion by Buddhist ideas. They were also of course the
questions of the Questing Beast.

Śaṅkara the Teacher

According to the tradition, Śaṅkara lived a brief and brilliant
life at the end of the eighth or the beginning of the ninth century A.D.* He is regarded with veneration as the great restorer
of Hinduism after the Buddhist era, the renewer of popular
religion as well as the profoundly learned interpreter of the
teaching of the Upanishads. He is believed to have traveled
extensively throughout India, founding the four *maths* referred
to earlier in the four corners of the subcontinent to continue his
teaching. He was certainly a metaphysical genius and a man of
profound spiritual experience, and had one clearly defined aim
in life, which he expresses in his description of the teacher
(Upad. 1.1.6):

> The teacher is one who possesses tranquility, self-control,
> and compassion and a desire to help others, who is versed

---

* Editor's note: Consensus now puts Śaṅkara a full century earlier,
at the beginning of the eighth century.

in the scriptures and unattached to enjoyments, seen and unseen . . . is a knower of Brahman and established in It. . . . He has the sole aim of helping others, and a desire to impart the knowledge of Brahman only.

The gist of his teaching is contained in the two following passages:

In the beginning this was being alone, one without a second . . . (Chānd. Up. Bh. 2.1):

The supreme transcendent Reality created the entire universe without help of any substance other than himself, and entered into all being for the sake of Self-realization. And having entered there he realized directly his own Self as "I am this Brahman." Therefore he is the only one Self in all bodies and there is none besides. And so everyone else too should realize thus: "He is my own Self"; "I am this Brahman." (Ait. Up. 2.1).

Śaṅkara was in fact confronted by the problem of the One and the Many in particularly acute form on account of his uncompromising acceptance of both the objective validity of the manifold given-in-experience at the level of our ordinary awareness, and the exigencies of his *ātmānubhava* or experience of the Self, fully corroborated by the insistence of scripture that Ātman-Brahman is not only one, but one-without-a-second, totally transcendent and untouched by any shadow of alteration. As Plato had already shown in a different cultural context, though a dialectical hierarchy of names and forms might prove satisfying from a purely logical point of view, it could not solve the existential problem of the chōrēsis or "gulf" between the Eternal and the non-eternal. In India, as in Greece, the ultimate question must always be that of the relation between the supreme unchanging Reality and the world of coming-to-be and passing away, the eternal Self and what appears as non-Self, and no epistemology can stand secure as long as this question remains unanswered.

RELATION AS THE KEY TO ŚAṄKARA'S THOUGHT

Father De Smet had offered me Śaṅkara's concept of relation as the key to his thought. As soon as I put it to the test I found that it turned easily in the lock. A systematic study of Śaṅkara's use of relational terms made it quite clear to me that he agrees with St. Thomas Aquinas in regarding the relation between creation and the ultimate Source of all being as a *non-reciprocal dependence relation,* i.e., a relation in which a subsistent effect or "relative absolute" is dependent on its cause for its very existence as a subsistent entity, whereas the cause is in no way dependent on the effect for its subsistence, though there is a necessary logical relation between cause and effect, i.e., a relation which is perceived by the mind when it reflects on the implications of the existence of the cosmos.

Śaṅkara has two characteristic terms to express this relation, *tādātmya,* the common dictionary rendering of which is "sameness or identity of nature or character with," and *ananyatva,* which most dictionaries translate as "identity." However, a close inspection of Śaṅkara's use of both terms suggests that the dictionary definitions are rather less subtle than strict accuracy demands—in fact, we have here two crucial examples of the linguistic problem referred to earlier.

Tādātmya

This term occurs seventeen times in the *Brahmasūtrabhāṣya* and twice in the small independent treatise, the *Upadeśasāhasrī* or *Thousand Teachings.* Literally the word means "having That as one's self," and it is used in the strict sense by Śaṅkara only to express the dependence of created beings upon the Ātman-Brahman. He employs it in an analogical and improper sense to describe the relation of one created being to another, but only insofar as one mediates to the other the creative power and agency of the supreme Self (Br.S. 2.4.19, Tait.Up.Bh. 2.2.1). His position on this point is well summed up in the following passages:

> Although one and the same Self is hidden in all beings, movable as well as immovable, yet owing to the gradual rise in excellence of the minds which form the limiting adjuncts [of the Self—i.e., the finite beings which appear to diversify it] scripture declares that the Self, though eternal, unchanging and uniform, reveals itself in a graduated series of beings, and so appears in forms of various dignity and power. (Br.S.Bh. 1.2.12)

> Thus golden ornaments and figures of gold are not identical with each other, but only in so far as gold constitutes the self of both. (Br.S.Bh. 4.1.4)

Again, even though Śaṅkara's favorite image of the *tādātmya* relationship in the phenomenal universe is the relation of materials such as gold or clay to the pots, ornaments, and so forth, fashioned of them, he is always keenly aware of a real distinction between the *upādāna karaṇa*, or inner cause—i.e., the clay, etc.—and its effects. The frequent rendering of *upādāna kāraṇa* into English as "material cause" inevitably leads to a blurring of this distinction and the labeling of Śaṅkara as a pantheist, whereas his whole effort is directed toward showing that while the effects of the Ātman-Brahman come to be and pass away, Ātman-Brahman suffers no shadow of change.

On their side, the "names and forms" or *upādhis* ("limiting adjuncts"), far from being stunted by their dependence on Ātman-Brahman, are constituted in relative autonomy and perfection precisely by that dependence: this is what is implied by saying that the ultimate Reality is the Self of every being. In echoing and explaining this Upanishadic phrase, Śaṅkara is in effect saying with the fourteenth-century English author of *The Scale of Perfection:* "He is thy Being, but thou art not his Being."

Ananyatva

I have checked every instance of *ananyatva*, literally "non-difference" or "not-otherness," and the adjectival form *ananya*, "not other" or "not different," in all the works of Śaṅkara generally accepted as authentic, and observed that they are always used of created or, as we should say, contingent being in relation to Ātman-Brahman, and never the other way round, i.e., of Ātman-Brahman in relation to created being. The "not-otherness" is clearly non-reciprocal, and in a passage in the Brahmasūtrabhāṣya which frequently seems to have been overlooked, Śaṅkara gives the clue to his usage: *ananyatva*, he says, means "not existing apart from." In other words, the identity is an identity with a difference—again an exact parallel to "He is thy Being, thou art not his Being."

Thus the supreme experience of man, the *anubhava* in which his ultimate end dawns upon him, is expressed in the Upanishadic "great saying" *Aham brahmāsmi,* "I am Brahman." On the other hand, "As long as one does not realize in this way this Self which has been described as 'Not this, not this' [i.e., by the apophatic way of transcendence], so long does one accept the limiting adjuncts [names and forms], body and so on, as one's proper self, and considering through ignorance these names and forms as intrinsic to the Self, one transmigrates under the influence of ignorance (*avidyā*), desire, and action" (Ait. Up. Bh., introduction). That is, without at least a glimmer of this *anubhava*, or realization of the supreme Absolute, it is impossible to be freed from our innate tendency to give an absolute value to some created thing, beginning with our limited selves, for without an absolute as point of reference, no human being can survive for long.

Śaṅkara offers no philosophical analysis or defense of his concept of the relation between Ātman-Brahman and created being such as we find in the theology of creation of Aquinas: he simply quotes the relevant scriptural passages and explains them sufficiently to make their implications clear for those seeking "a way of salvation through knowledge." Anyone interested in pursuing the question further should refer to A. Krempel on St. Thomas's concept of relation.[1] I am confident that Śaṅkara would have endorsed Thomas's extremely lucid exposition of the relation between God and creation and accepted it as a valid authentication of his own position. However, like Aquinas, Śaṅkara was not primarily a philosopher. He was a theologian, in the original connotation of that term as one who not only *learns* but *experiences* divine things—in the really untranslatable phrase of the pseudo-Denys, "*non solum discens sed patiens divina.*"[2] Without grasping this it is impossible even to glimpse the true meaning of advaita as he understood it.

This is perhaps the place to add that Śaṅkara nowhere tries to explain the exact nature of the creative "act" which gives rise to the relation of dependence he discusses. He simply quotes scripture, stresses its essential gratuitousness and effortlessness and the fact that it in no way touches the transcendence of Brahman, and leaves it at that.

THE THEOLOGICAL TASK:
A NON-DUALIST PERSPECTIVE

It is essential to remember that, as already noted, for Śaṅkara, theology or "enquiry into Brahman"—*brahmajijñāsā,* equally legitimately (and significantly) translated as "the desire to know Brahman"—is by no means a merely intellectual exercise: it is an adventure which involves the whole of one's being and presupposes a total self-commitment (cf. Br.S.Bh. 1.1.1 and Upad. 1.2). Its subjective starting-point is twofold: the all-consuming desire to "know Brahman" and a concomitant recognition that while there is a radical distinction between the ephemeral and the eternal, there is in man an innate tendency to confuse them—in other words, a realization that there is something basically wrong with the human condition for which "knowledge of Brahman" is the remedy.

Therefore, if the fledgling theologian is to hope for any success in his task, he must begin by establishing order as far as possible in his own person in relation to Brahman. Hence he requires the other traditional prerequisites for theologizing, of which the first is, *śraddhā* or faith, "the abdication by reason of any claim to self-sufficiency in the matter of supreme knowledge." The saving knowledge of Brahman is pure gift, available only through *śruti* or scripture[3] and *anubhava* or experience, for which the help of a guru is normally necessary. This leads to the second prerequisite, *śravaṇa*, or listening to the scriptures and the guru. The disciple must also reflect on the meaning of *śruti* (*manana*) and develop his power of discrimination or discernment between the ephemeral and the eternal, be freed from attachment to the enjoyment of anything less than Brahman, both in this life and after death, and have a quiet mind, self-control, renunciation, perseverance, and power of concentration. Finally, prayer is absolutely essential: "The understanding of the True cannot be acquired unless it is sought for and prayed for: hence he says, "This understanding itself one must seek to understand" (Chānd. Up. Bh. 7.17.1).

This Self that has been explained and whose attainment is the highest human goal is not attained through extensive study of Vedas and scripture, similarly not through intelligence, the power of retention of the meaning of the texts, nor through much hearing. By what then can it be reached? This is being explained. That very entity, the supreme Self, which this one, the man of knowledge, seeks to attain, is attainable by that very fact of hankering, but not through any other spiritual effort, for it is by its very nature ever attained. This Self of his reveals its own supreme nature (as the Self of his own limited self), its reality that was enveloped in ignorance. The idea is that when knowledge dawns, the Self becomes revealed, just like pots, etc., on the coming of light. Thus the meaning is that the means for the attaining of the Self consists in praying for this consummation to the exclusion of everything else. (Muṇḍ. Up. Bh. 3.2.3)

Śaṅkara lists quite bluntly what he calls "causes of non-comprehension" on the part of the student of theology: "past and present sins, laxity, want of previous firm knowledge of what constitutes the subject of discrimination between the eternal and the non-eternal, courting popular esteem, vanity of caste, etc." It may seem to us paradoxical to suggest that there could be a connection between, let us say, chain-smoking, drinking, or addictive light reading, vanity or gossip, and lack of theological insight: Śaṅkara would have found no paradox.

The demands on a teacher of theology already quoted are naturally no less taxing:

The teacher is one who is endowed with the power of furnishing arguments pro and con, of understanding questions and remembering them, who possesses self-control, tranquility, compassion, and a desire to help others, who is versed in the scriptures and unattached to enjoyments both seen and unseen; who has renounced the means to all kinds of actions, is a knower of Brahman and established in it, who is devoid of shortcomings such as ostentation, deceit, cunning, pride, jugglery, jealousy, falsehood, egotism, and attachment. He has the sole aim of helping others and a desire to impart the knowledge of Brahman only. (Upad. 1.1.6)

Theology therefore implies a total dedication on the part of both teacher and taught, and it consists in a steady endeavour to "know Brahman" not as an object "out there" but as a "non-object" (*aviṣaya*), the Self of one's own self and of all other beings.

The Object of Theology

After what has just been said it may seem paradoxical to speak of an "object" of advaitic theology, and in fact as Abhishik-tananda pointed out, in the Upanishads the *brahmavid* or knower of Brahman is more accurately described as *evamvid*, the man who "knows *thus*": as the Kena Upanishad puts it, Brahman is "not that which one knows," but that by which one knows as though a crystal bowl were aware of the sun shining through it. "When he is known through all cognitions, he is rightly known." The final goal of *brahmajijñāsā* is not Brahman conceptually known—an impossible task—but Brahman experienced as beyond all conceptual knowledge. This has obvious resonances with wisdom in the biblical tradition and the apophatic tradition in Christian mystical theology. However, within the sphere of conceptual knowledge, for Śaṅkara as for St. Thomas, the task of theology is to "set things in order," to borrow, significantly enough, Aristotle's phrase for the specific task of the wise man: to establish order in our worldview by recognizing that Brahman is "the Mystery from which the birth, etc., of the universe derives"—the source, sustainer and goal of all things—and that, rightly seen, every other being is simply a "name and form," a subsistent but ephemeral manifestation of that Mystery on the "coming to be and passing away" level. This is in fact the truth of the universe and of human existence, the knowledge which dispels ignorance, that tendency to confusion and to absolutizing of the relative, which seems to be inherent in man's nature, recognition of which is one of the subjective starting-points for theological enquiry. From this standpoint, theology prepares the way for that moment of awakening, its crown and consummation, which one cannot precipitate for oneself but only prepare for by self-discipline and pray for with all one's heart.

The Source of Theology

Śaṅkara gives two possible interpretations of the key text of the Brahmasūtras on the source of theology: "*śāstrayonitvāt*" (Br. S. 1.1.3), namely, "Brahman is the source [i.e., the cause] of Scripture," and "Scripture is the source or cause [i.e., the means] of right knowledge" through which we understand the nature of Brahman. Thus, the sense would be "through scripture alone as the source of knowledge Brahman is known as the cause of the origin, etc., of this world."

This last sentence is extremely important for a proper understanding of Śaṅkara: *formaliter*, we can theologize only in the light of *śruti*, because it is only by this light that we can know that Brahman is the source of the universe, origin, sustainer, and end of all things, the self of every being, and also that "creation" exists solely for the sake of the Self-realization of Brahman in and through it, though "creation" is at the same time wholly gratuitous and in no way necessary to Brahman (Br. S. Bh. 2.1.33) any more than the sun needs a pool in which it is reflected.

In the last analysis, *anubhava* or experience is also necessary, but *śruti* provides as it were the content of *anubhava*: "cessation of all mental activity which culminates simply in elimination of knowledge of the non-Self is not the same as *brahmavidyā*, for it reveals nothing. It must be preceded by a positive ascertaining of the supreme Self as Fullness of being. This can only be done under the guidance of scripture, through the great sayings *tattvamasi* ('That art Thou') and *aham brahmāsmi* ('I am Brahman') as well as *neti, neti* ('not this, not this')" (cf. Upad. 2.18.124, 127; also 9–12, 105–106, 122).[4]

But the enquiry into Brahman also involves rational reflection or *manana*. Śaṅkara explicitly insists that in every sphere but the knowledge of Brahman as such, human intelligence is perfectly capable of arriving at true knowledge through perception and inference: *śruti* is competent within its own sphere, but not outside it, precisely because the other *pramāṇas* or means of knowledge are also competent within their own spheres. The logical inference from this is that if Śaṅkara does not give much attention to such questions as the nature of the individual self and the created world, this is not because he regards them as "illusory" and certainly not as nonexistent, but because they can be known by ordinary human means. It is, he says, "The Lord, about whom ordinary experience tells us nothing, who is to be considered as the special topic of all *śrutis*" (Br.S. 1.3.7), and he himself was especially concerned to stress the transcendence and "one-without a-second" character of Brahman to counteract the Sāṃkhya teaching which compromised this, as already noted.

It appears perfectly lawful to conclude both from his own example and from what he says here that Śaṅkara regarded everyday experience, his own and other people's, as essential input for *brahmajijñāsā* inasmuch as we have to start from where we are in our own awareness of the cosmic situation. But if our search is to be *brahmajijñāsā* it must be done in the light of *śruti*. Although through purely rational reflection on the world and the individual self we can reach the conclusion that they demand a sufficient cause or ground for their existence, it is only through *śruti* that we can know that this cause or ground is Brahman or the Self (There seems to be an interesting parallel here with St. Thomas Aquinas's comment at the end of three of his five ways of enquiring into the existence of God: "this *we are accustomed to call* God"[5]).

The Method of *Brahmajijñāsā*

Brahman is known from *śruti* "because it is their import." Therefore the seeker, having firmly committed himself to the supreme goal of human existence with his whole mind and heart and strength, and having as far as possible set his own house in order by the means already described, must devote himself to *śravaṇa* or listening to the words of *śruti*, normally under the guidance of a teacher. "*Śravaṇa* necessitates a guru. A guru is like a boat on that great ocean of *saṃsāra* (worldly existence)" (Br. Up. Bh. 1.4.9; cf. Muṇḍ. Up. Bh. 1.2.21). It includes exegesis according to the six rules of interpretation laid down by the founder of the Mīmāṃsā school of philosophy, "the ascertainment by the six indications that the Brahman, one without a second, is the final purport of all the Upanishads" (*Vedāntasāra*, lines 10, 11). This is followed by reflection with the help of the other means of knowledge in support of the teaching of *śruti*, and finally *nididhyāsana*, the silent assimilation of the teaching: "the highest form of knowledge, which consists in abiding constantly in the Self, bearing in mind that the Self is all and that nothing else is really existent" (Bh. G. Bh. 6.25—"really existent," in the sense of being absolutely self-sufficient and unchanging, self-existent). This process is to be repeated until *brahmavidyā* or knowledge of the supreme Reality dawns. Śaṅkara allows that some especially "quick-witted" and well-prepared disciples may come to *brahmavidyā* at the first hearing of a *mahāvākya*, or "great saying,"[6] but this is not normal. Usually "repetition" and *manana* are needed, but Śaṅkara insists that awareness of the gratuitousness of the gift must be safeguarded at all costs; obviously, for the transcendence of Brahman is at stake: "For him who does not reach that intuition (*anubhava*) we admit repetition, so that the desired intuition may be brought about. He however must not be brought to repetition in such a way as to make him lose the true sense of 'That art thou.' In the mind of the one on whom repetition is enjoined as a duty, there arise infallibly notions that are opposed to the true knowledge of Brahman, such as 'I have a right to this knowledge as an agent, this is to be done by me'" (Br. S. Bh. 4.1.2).

A peculiarly characteristic element in this process seems to be the *nididhyāsana* stage, the silent sitting without "running around" of the discursive mind, simply allowing a key sentence of scripture to sink into possession of one's whole being until the awakening comes from within:

Of it there is this teaching:
That in the lightning which flashes forth, which makes one say "Ah":—That "Ah" refers to divinity (it is *adhidaivatam*).

Now with regard to oneself:
That which comes to the mind, by which one repeatedly remembers—that conception (*saṃkalpa*, impression) is It. (Kaṭh. Up. 4.29, 30).
Once that Self is known, everything else is known. (Br. Up. Bh. 4.1.6). It is known through all cognitions (Kaṭh. Up).

This liberating knowledge includes all other knowledge; it does not, however, "destroy" the universe or even the awareness of it through other *pramāṇas*, except in moments of great intensity: it only dispels the illusion that it is the ultimate reality (Br. S. Bh. 3.2.21). It eliminates all lesser goals unrelated to the attainment of the supreme Self, for it is the fulfillment of all desires (Br. Up. Bh. 4.4.8). "It gives one the conviction that one is completely blessed, and it requires no other witness than the testimony of one's own experience" (Br. Up. Bh. 4.4.8). "The knower of Brahman enjoys all desires, all delights procured by the desirable objects without exception. Does he enjoy sons, heaven, etc., alternately as we do? No, he enjoys all delectable things simultaneously, as amassed together in a single moment through a single perception which is eternal, like the light of the sun, which is non-different from the essence of Brahman and which we have described as Reality-Knowledge-Infinite. . . . He enjoys all things by that Brahman whose nature is omniscience" (Tait. Up. Bh. 2.1.1).

Beatitudo est gaudium de veritate, says St. Thomas Aquinas—
"perfect happiness is joy in truth." Long before it had com-
pleted its doctoral studies the Questing Beast had verified in
its own being, beyond all possibility of doubt, the truth of
Dante's words quoted at the beginning of my first lecture: "I
see well that our intellect is never sated until that True enlightens it, outside of which no truth has space. In that it reposes,
like a beast in its lair, as soon as it gains it: and *gain it it can, else
every desire were in vain.*"

Śaṅkara and Aquinas

At this point it may be useful to make a brief comparison of
Śaṅkara and St. Thomas Aquinas from the point of view of both
what they have in common and the difference between them.
First, what they have in common:

1. Both were theologians and men of very deep spiritual experience. Their starting-point was their own faith, *"patiens, non
   solum discens,"* in a supreme Mystery which had taken the
   absolutely free initiative of creation and of making, through
   certain privileged individuals, a Self-communication to
   human beings which was at first transmitted orally and later
   committed to writing. Their prime concern was to know that
   Mystery in its own true nature and to help their fellow-men
   and women to reach salvation through the same transforming and beatifying knowledge.
2. Both held that the content of this Self-communication consisted in a revelation of the nature of the Mystery, both in
   itself and as the ultimate goal of human existence, which
   was otherwise inaccessible to man left to his own resources.
3. Both were convinced that this Mystery was the Source and
   Ground of the extramental universe and of the individual
   self, and that some valid knowledge of it insofar as it was
   their Ground and cause could be gained through them as its

effects, but both also held that man could not know that the Ground of the universe thus apprehended was the same reality made known through revelation except through revelation itself.

4. Both held that while Self-communication of the Mystery was to be received by man as something wholly given, to which he could make no claim as an agent in his own right, it was nevertheless right and proper for him to satisfy himself that this revelation was in harmony with the evidence of the other sources of knowledge he was endowed with.

5. As a logical consequence, both recognized and respected the legitimate autonomy of other branches of knowledge based upon such evidence.

6. For both, therefore, there was no fundamental conflict or contradiction between the sphere of revelation and the sphere of everyday life: in their lives as in their teaching, both exemplified the axiom beloved of Thomas that "Truth cannot contradict Truth."

7. Both were non-dualists, understanding the relation of the universe, including individual selves, to uncreated Being in terms of a non-reciprocal relation of dependence which, far from diminishing the uniqueness and lawful autonomy of a created being within its own sphere, was their necessary Ground and condition, while apart from that relation of total dependence no created being would *be* at all.

8. Their theologies therefore issue naturally in a holistic and practical spirituality singularly suited to our times: for both, the truly "realized" man or woman is the person whose whole being has been brought into such inner harmony that every thought, word, or deed is the expression of the Indweller, the Mystery in which each one lives and moves and has their being, and who can therefore freely recognize that same Presence as the Self of all other human beings, since this revelation is no longer blocked or clouded by disordered personal fears or desires.

9. Nevertheless, both recognized that, de facto, there is a great disorder both in man as an individual and, as a result, in human society. The root of this disorder both traced, in terms of their own traditions, to a tendency somehow inherent in man's condition as a finite being to refuse to accept the limitations of his creaturehood. To remedy this situation was for both beyond man's unaided power, yet both believed that it could be remedied, "else every desire were in vain."

Though there is such fundamental agreement between Śaṅkara and Thomas, there is also a difference of emphasis which is no less illuminating for us—a difference which not surprisingly is found also in their respective traditions, nondualist Vedānta and Christianity. Both are intensely aware of the dependence of creation on the Mystery beyond name and form without which it would simply not exist at all: both are nevertheless keenly aware that the creation is very much "there"—relative, indeed, but ineluctably to be reckoned with. At the same time it is undeniably true that while reading Śaṅkara the "searcher into majesty" is so "overwhelmed with glory," as the Imitation of Christ puts it, that his own finite selfhood fades into insignificance—so much so that even today it remains an open question whether or not Śaṅkara personally believed in the ultimate survival of the individual as such. Most commentators would probably say he did not.

In Thomas, on the other hand, what holds the attention is the flowing-out (*emanatio*) and return of creatures from and to God their Source and End, in all their rich diversity, and always in the background, like the muted roar of some great river in spate, is the awareness that both flowing forth and return are enfolded in the "coming forth" and "returning" of the eternal Word in whom all things were created and continue to subsist and who himself "became flesh" and dwelt as a man among men, "for the life of the world."

This difference, however, should probably not be exaggerated: toward the end of his life, Thomas too was so overwhelmed by the depth of the revelation given to him that he could no longer concentrate on "names and forms," even to the extent of leaving his greatest work unfinished. In a way, the difference only serves to throw into great relief the extraordinary agreement between the two men, deep calling to deep across the centuries, and the cultural barriers in a twofold harmony which ultimately springs from the same root, the profoundly simple and self-validating experience of non-duality. For both Śaṅkara and Thomas, Being and being are not one in an absolutely monistic sense, as a man and his shadow are not one, but they are not absolutely two either, for each could have made his own the statement of the fourteenth-century English mystic already quoted: "He is thy Being, but thou are not his being."

The same point of complementarity through difference of stress can be made rather differently by saying that the Gospel lived radically leads straight to advaita, or, from the other angle, that the perfect practical handbook for living out advaita is the Gospel.

In the light of this comparison, does it still make sense to speak of "the challenge" of advaita? Must its significance for us be reduced to a simple exhortation to return to the study of St. Thomas with a greater alertness to the apophatic dimension of his theology?

From my own personal experience, I do not think so. I have found and still find that the advaita of the Upanishads and of Śaṅkara challenges my Christian "faith seeking understanding" in three ways, all of which I think are relevant to the Churches in today's world:

1. By its uncompromising insistence and spelling out in detail of the demands the theological quest makes on a human being; one cannot "do" theology as one may "do" mathe-

matics or history or any other branch of academic study. Unless our life-style and value-systems are in harmony with the demands of the Truth we are pursuing, we cannot hope for real enlightenment.

2. By the starkly apophatic character of the Upanishadic teaching regarding the Supreme, a dimension which has been heavily overlaid in Christian tradition in recent centuries and yet appeals so strongly to modern man, starved of transcendence and mystery; the keen sense of this absolute transcendence and the relative non-being of all created things which the so-called "advaitic experience" opens up to shatter our comfortable self-assurance. I think that, paradoxically perhaps, our generation needs this experience both to counterbalance our easy assumption of the all-importance of this world and also to give us back a sense of hope in an ultimate meaning for our daily lives beyond the range of our present mental grasp. We hear much less today of heaven, hell, purgatory, and judgement than in the past because, one suspects, no one knows what to say of them any more; there is a real crisis of credibility in this area. Perhaps we need a reminder that, as Paul well knew, "eye has not seen nor ear heard nor has it entered into the heart of man" what God has in preparation for us. A firm and trusting admission of agnosticism might go far to stem the tide of disillusionment created by taking for granted, as still sufficient for us today, the myths and symbols which satisfied older and less scientifically sophisticated generations than our own, who, moreover, recognized them for what they were—myths and symbols which had to be transcended. Too often today they are regarded simply as fairy tales. The advaitic approach could, I think, help us towards a far more realist eschatology as well as a powerful reaffirmation of the apophatic dimension of Christian faith.

3. By the Copernican revolution which would be brought about in our theological expression of our faith if we adopted as

our basis the experience of "God" as the immanent yet transcendent Self instead of the "God up there" or "out there" of traditional imagery, to whom contemporary man finds it increasingly hard to relate. We have to face the fact that acceptance of either a heaven or a God "up there" is no longer culturally or theologically possible. Theology needs to be reborn in every age and culture in terms of contemporary human experience. It is in fact born of reflection on this experience in the light of faith and of the faith-experience of earlier generations. Formulations of faith which we can recognize as perfectly valid in terms of the universe of discourse of the generation or culture which evolved them frequently do not speak to a later age or different culture, and may even serve as blocks to the communication of the living message of the Gospel. I think, and I speak from fairly considerable experience, that the non-dualist tradition of Hinduism could help us to find a universally viable alternative for today—one which would enable us to transcend the cultural and religious barriers that divide us without destroying the rich treasure of our diversities.

Notes

1. A. Krempel, *La Doctrine de la Relation chez Saint Thomas*, Librarie Philosophique J. Vrin (Paris, 1952).

2. I have called Śaṅkara a theologian as distinct from a philosopher insofar as he took as his ultimate authority not human reason but the revelation enshrined in *śruti*. Whether or not he can justly be described as a theist is matter for debate.

3. This very specific claim of the Vedic tradition to a revealed knowledge otherwise inaccessible to human reason and embodied in the texts of *śruti* offers a potentially very enriching challenge to the Churches.

4. A number of modern practitioners of meditation have come to grief because the "cessation of all mental activity" has led them into a contentless void. I know of at least one case of attempted suicide. Teachers of transcendental meditation and other "contentless" methods of meditation might do well to ponder Śaṅkara's advice here.

5. S. Thomas Aquinas, *Summa Theologica* Part 1, q. 2, a. 3. Almost the same phrase is used in the two following proofs.

6. The *mahāvākya* are a small group of texts, including *aham brahmāsmi*, "I am Brahman," and *tattvamasi*, "That art thou," regarded as especially efficacious in "awakening" the duly prepared disciple to the supreme knowledge.

Theologizing from an Alternative Experience

◜━━━━◞

At the end of all our knowing we know God as something unknown:
we are united with him as with something wholly unknown.
—St. Thomas Aquinas

As I attempted to put my thoughts in order for this final lecture I realized that if theology may be defined in a broad sense as reflection on experience in the light of faith, the Questing Beast had been engaged in rudimentary theological reflection almost from birth.[1] I further realized that this had been a process of discernment in both the Indian and the Ignatian senses of the term. I remembered the words of two wise and holy men, both now dead: our music panditji in Pune once said to me, quoting the *Jñāneshwari,* the great Marathi commentary on the Bhagavad Gītā, "My Guru is within my heart, he is the *viveka* (power of discernment) within my heart," thereby completing the brief and brilliant summary of the teaching of St. Ignatius on discernment given to me a few years before by Father James Walsh, S.J., in which he stressed the importance of "consolations and desolations" and a peaceful sense of consonance with the habitual leading of God in one's life as indications of the true path, rather than intellectual weighing of pros and cons (though this too has its place). I saw very clearly that although as time went on I had the great good fortune of being given a very solid intellectual foundation for my reflection, the compass bearings and the pilot light for my "questing" had indeed been provided on the one hand by the sense of joy or discomfort by which "his unction teaches us all things," and on the other by an ongoing awareness that there can never be real theological insight without a steady accompanying effort at integrity of heart and discipline of life.

I think it is important to stress this here because ever since the Modernist crisis in relation to theology, and for several centuries before that in the realm of prayer and spirituality, as I noted in my first lecture, the invocation of experience as a criterion of truth has officially been regarded with some suspicion, with disastrous consequences to both individuals and to the Church. It is obviously true that we cannot jettison "the tradition handed down by the apostles" in favor of private inspiration, but as the Vatican Council fathers reminded us, this same tradition "develops in the Church with the help of the Holy Spirit. For there is a growth in the understanding of the realities and the words which have been handed down. This happens through the *contemplation and study of believers who treasure these things in their hearts* (cf. Lk. 2:19, 51) . . . [and] through the *intimate understanding of spiritual things they experience* . . . [as well as] through the preaching of those who have received through episcopal succession the sure gift of truth. For, as the centuries succeed one another, the Church constantly moves forward towards the fulness of divine truth, until the words of God reach their complete fulfilment in her" (*Dei Verbum,* no. 8). In our days especially, when such vast possibilities are opening up of growth in human knowledge and of contact and mutual understanding between people of different faiths and cultures, it is crucially important for the Church to encourage all her members to bring the light of faith to bear on these encounters in order to come to a deeper penetration into the mystery of Christ, if she is not only to be true to the mission entrusted to her to "make known the secret hidden from eternity in God" of which Paul spoke to the Ephesians, but even to preserve her credibility in the eyes of a generation increasingly impatient with a narrowly fundamentalist or exclusivist approach in religion and spirituality.[2]

In this connection two other conciliar texts are extremely relevant, both from the Decree on Ecumenism. The first urges all members of the Church to "preserve a proper freedom . . . *even in the theological elaboration of revealed truth*" (no. 4). The second adds that "if the influence of events or of the times has led to deficiencies . . . *even in the formulation of doctrine,* these should be *appropriately rectified* at the proper moment" (no. 6). In both these situations it would seem that the "consolations and desolations" of serious believers in living and frequent contact with the changing realities of the human condition could be valuable pointers to the areas in which modification and development are needed.

It is in these perspectives that my community has lived and pondered for almost twenty years, offering the fruits of our experience and reflection to the local Church from time to time through our participation in seminars, pastoral conferences, and informal exchange, for feedback and checking of our bearings. Before saying anything more about our reflection as a community, however, it may be useful to pause for a moment and briefly summarize my own theological state of mind when in 1972 I became one of the first members of the reopened Christa Prema Seva Ashram.

THE ONGOING CHALLENGE OF ADVAITA

When I first came to Pune I had just finished my doctoral studies and in a sense come to terms with the advaita of Śaṅkarācārya, but I still found myself seriously challenged regarding traditional formulations of Christian faith on the following points, some of which I mentioned briefly at the end of my second lecture:

1. The serene and still normal assumption that Christianity is *the* (only) revealed religion, for Śaṅkara is just as serenely assured that "the enquiry into Brahman" must begin by an act of faith in a Self-manifestation of Brahman gratuitously given to man; it actually begins, he says, "with an abdication by reason of any claim to self-sufficiency in the realm of supreme knowledge. Indeed, reason begins here with an act of faith in the exclusive authority of a given testimony concerning the proper nature of the Transcendent" (Br. S. Bh. 2.1.15).

2. Our dualistic way of thinking and speaking about God as somehow "over against" us, as an ultimate Object or even "Thou."[3]

3. Our manner of thinking of baptism and the gift of the Spirit as though God somehow "came in from outside," as it were, and were not already present " in" us by the very fact of our being at all. Christian theology has always known this, but somehow the presence in all things "by essence, presence and power" seems rarely to have been satisfactorily related to the economy of grace. (This was of course one of the great problems of the Questing Beast, as of St. Teresa of Avila in an earlier age.)

4. Traditional attempts to formulate the mystery of the Incarnation: what exactly does it mean to say "Jesus is God"? What difference would there be in the "great saying" or *mahāvākya* "I am Brahman" as uttered by him and the same sentence as uttered by an "ordinary" realized man? What is our relation, as "sons in the Son," to Jesus, to God?

5. Our continued use of the term "person"[4] in speaking of the inner dynamism of the Godhead and the usual presenta-

tion of the "Fall" and redemption of man, original sin, and life "after" death.

6. Our present tendency, in reaction against the excessively "world-negating" spiritualities of the past, to repudiate the apophatic element in Christian tradition characteristic of the Fathers and Christian mystics of all ages, and so "absolutize" creation to the extent of at least appearing to subordinate the ultimate Mystery to man and to proclaim this subordination as an essential differentiating characteristic of Christianity.

Obviously, Christian thought-patterns have been challenged on these and other points from other quarters too, but so far as advaita is concerned the challenges all stem from the radically different metaphysical assumption underlying them, namely, that the tendency to "objectify" the ultimate Mystery and identify it with "names and forms" of any kind whatever is the root of all error and therefore of all evil. For both the Questing Beast and the Tamil saint Sadashiva, it was the root of all spiritual alienation in an apparently dualistic world, as it must be for anyone who has begun to apprehend, however dimly, that "in every 'I' which I attempt to utter, his 'I' is already glowing."

THE ASHRAM COMMUNITY

In this place, openness to other religions springs from commitment to Christ.
    —Dr. M. M. Thomas, referring to the C. P.S. Ashram, Pune

The starting point of our theological reflection as a community was determined by the nature of the community itself, and especially by the central role of the risen Christ in our life. As I said at the end of my first lecture, we entered into an already existing tradition, in that the ashram had been founded in 1927 by an Anglican priest, Father Jack Winslow, with a view to counteracting the long-standing and then still prevailing habit of Western missionaries of introducing their own culture with the Gospel, and so contributing to the alienation of Indian Christians from their own sociocultural and spiritual inheritance. Father Winslow was a personal friend of Mahatma Gandhi, who stayed in the ashram more than once, and this had a profound influence on the ideas and life-style of the community, as we found when we were gladly adopted as a "little Sister" by the Brahma Vidyā Mandir Ashram at Paunar, founded by Vinoba Bhave to give women access to *brahmavidyā*, "the knowledge of Brahman," traditionally regarded as a male prerogative. The first community was in profound sympathy with the Independence movement and open to all that was not incompatible with the Gospel in Hinduism and the other great religions of India, studying their scriptures and, as far as they could, incorporating Indian ways of worship.[5] Among its members were the Rev. C.F. Andrews, Verrier Elwin, the anthropologist, and Father Algy Roberts, later co-founder in England of the Anglican Franciscan community. Bishop William Lash of Bombay was one of the last *ācāryas*, and the Indian Catholic artist Angelo de Fonseca found in the ashram a congenial home for sixteen years. The ashram thus had both Indian and English members, including some Catholics, but was not specifically ecumenical, though it welcomed members of all (Churches) as well as all faiths.

This first community came to an end in the 1960s, and when the ashram was reopened in 1972 under the auspices of Bishop Christopher Robinson, chairman of the board of trustees, it was deliberately ecumenical, with Anglican and Catholic, and later Evangelical, members of the core community, as well as a wise and spiritual elderly Hindu lady. This was extremely important from the theological point of view because from the beginning we had to concentrate on what we had in common as Christians, and the Gospel naturally became the common basis and practical handbook for our community life. We also learnt from the start to listen with Hindu ears to the psalms and other readings from the Bible whenever our Hindu member was present, which opened our eyes to many things: "all the gods of the nations are devils," for example, or with regard to idols, "having eyes they see not—having ears they hear not. May those who worship them become like them." Was this really what the Spirit was saying in India today? How were we to understand these texts?

The ashram tradition, wide and flexible as it is, also had a powerful determining influence on our life and thought, not only because of its radical simplicity so much in harmony with the Gospel, but because of the necessity of coming to terms with the question of the guru; we fairly soon came to the conclusion that the only possible guru for us was the risen Lord, with a human leader as visible "facilitator" for his Spirit living in each member. Gradually we found that more and more people, of all religions and none, were coming from all over India, Asia, and the world to stay for longer or shorter periods, so in order to make it clear from the beginning what kind of a place this was we put up a poster near the entrance which states for all to read:

> The Guru of this ashram is the risen Christ, present among us by his Spirit and by Word and Sacrament. A central concern of the community is to reflect on and enter more deeply into the mystery of the relation of Christ to the Self-communication of God in and through the other great spiritual traditions of the world. High points of this endeavor are the daily Eucharist and meditation hours, the *arati* times (morning, midday, and evening prayer), and the *satsangs*.

Visitors are invited to share in this search, which has such significance for the world of our times, and so to help to make this place a true "crossroads of the Spirit."

Normally the household numbers from twenty to thirty in all, with about twelve long-term members, including a core group of five or six. Though in the nature of things we cannot insist on everyone taking part in our worship, everyone knows that they are welcome to join in whatever is going on in the ashram except the weekly community meetings. Quite often people do come to the Eucharist or *arati,* including many from a Christian background who have been out of touch with Christianity for years, and there is much frank and free discussion at the *satsangs* and "meeting-points," arranged by request, where some basic text—an Upanishad, a Gospel, the Yoga Sūtras of Patañjali, the Bhagavad-Gītā—is taken as basis for wide-ranging reflection. From time to time we have groups of students, seminarians, sisters, and lay people for "ashram experience." The ashram lifestyle lends itself to relaxed and friendly relationships: everyone helps with some household task, according to capacity, and there is no distinction of caste or creed, rich or poor—those who come asking for food sit with us in our open-verandah dining-place. We are allowed to live in the ashram rent-free by the trustees, but though we have no endowments and rely on goodwill offerings from those who come to cover running costs, we never refuse anyone who cannot give, and the Lord somehow provides. We have no institutional work, and our ministry as community is simply to share our life with all comers, "at the service of the love of Christ," as the name of the ashram puts it.

In this situation we very soon found ourselves compelled to face some extremely down-to-earth and practical questions about what the Gospel demanded of us. In what follows I shall concentrate mainly on those which touch the central concern of this lecture—namely, the need for "theological elaboration of revealed truth" in terms which are more intelligible to the men and women of our time exposed to the sometimes intoxicating or profoundly unsettling experience of "interreligious conversation," as a recent writer in the English *Tablet* aptly put it. It seems important, however, to stress that our theological reflection is only one expression of a habitual reference to the Gospel as criterion for action.[6]

The Starting Point

Paradoxically enough, given our ecumenical character, the daily celebration of the Eucharist has always been the center of our lives as community, the source of our union, and the never-failing renewer of inspiration and strength. In view of the divisions between our Churches, it is true that we had to work through great anguish and grope for mutual understanding at the beginning, because of the differences which we all feel bound to respect and which are still associated with deep emotions. Such emotions are most keenly felt as we sit around the Lord's table and cannot share full and equal participation. However, perhaps the very effort we had to put into this, combined with the sympathetic comprehension of our bishops, helped us to come through to our present sense of deep union of mind and heart as we accept the hard reality of where our Churches are and pray that "full and *visible* union may soon be established among us all Christians."[7]

In 1972 the Catholic Church in India was in the full tide of liturgical renewal, to which Vatican II had given a great impetus. Centers for "experimentation" were set up, and we were one of the first of these. This meant that we had a certain freedom with regard to the use of Indian ways of worship and even the use of other scriptures in our liturgy. Some years later this permission was temporarily withdrawn,[8] but almost simultaneously the Liturgy Committee of the Church of North India recognized us as an official experimental group with a mandate to evolve a more Indian way of celebration of the Eucharist. (A presbyter of the Church of North India, the Rev. Yesudas Tiwari, was at that time a member of our community.) The CNI gave us even more freedom than the Catholic Church, which we made good use of when Father Yesudas celebrated. We continued to read a passage from other scriptures every day that "resonated" with the biblical readings, but did this in a preparatory paraliturgy, as the Catholic bishops no longer allowed other scriptures to be read during the Liturgy of the Word.

In this early period we drew great inspiration from a passage of the Vatican Council document on the Church in the Modern World: "Since Christ died for all men, and the vocation of man is in fact one and divine, we ought to believe that the Holy Spirit, in ways known only to God, offers to every man the possibility of being associated with this paschal mystery" (no. 22). Gradually we built up a certain familiarity with the main Hindu scriptures and *bhakti* tradition, and to a lesser extent with Islam.[9] The extremely positive findings of the research seminar held at the National Biblical Catechetical and Liturgical Centre, Bangalore, in December 1974 on non-biblical scriptures and their use in Christian worship encouraged us greatly, particularly the strong affirmation that the liturgical celebration is the setting *par excellence* for reflection on the mystery of Christ in the light of both biblical and non-biblical scriptures.

THE EASTER VIGIL

From the beginning, the high point of the year for us has been Holy Week, the celebration of the passion, death, and resurrection of our Lord. Ever since 1972, when we had with us both Swami Abhishiktananda and our Hindu Panditji, whom we had first met at Paunar, we have tried to keep in mind the Indian context—both the presence and action of the Spirit in other traditions down the ages and the contemporary situation of the country.

Here we found ourselves faced in an even more acute form by a problem we met to some extent every day as we "searched the scriptures" for complementary readings—the problem of finding a common basis or "universe of discourse." In its most elementary terms this problem arose from the fact that whereas biblical tradition and Christian faith are rooted in history, and their historical character is essential to their identity, Hinduism has no such preoccupation with history. Its main concern is man's relation to the Eternal expressed through myth and symbol, which are seen as essentially relevant for all times and places. Whether Lord Krishna was a historical figure or not is of no great importance to the devout Hindu, and even though today, with India's growing consciousness of having a significant role in world affairs and the spread of modern ways of thought and living, there are attempts to trace historical roots for Krishna as for Rama, it remains true that the events of the Gospel and the Bhagavad-Gītā, for example, are on quite different planes of reality.[10]

Another aspect of the "universe of discourse" problem is that of language, made more acute by the inadequate knowledge of Hinduism of some earlier translators of scriptural and liturgical texts; for example, the Hindi word *swarga* used to render "heaven" conveys the idea of a place of very earthly joy, a kind of transit-lounge for those who have led good earthly lives but have not attained the degree of purification necessary for complete liberation from the cycles of birth and death. Similarly, the word "God" in English is used by Christians to mean both God in his inaccessible mystery and God as Creator and Lord of heaven and earth, whereas traditionally Hindus never use the same words for both aspects of the supreme Mystery. This has led many Hindus to think that Christians know nothing of the apophatic approach to the Eternal. The difficulty of course is to know what precise meaning one's use of language is conveying to others, and how accurately one is understanding them.

We wrestled with this problem of the "universe of discourse" for years. It was not until 1988 that we felt we had made a final breakthrough, though each year there was some small advance in comprehension.

The general outline of our Easter Vigils has always been determined by the liturgical texts of the Catholic Church and of the Church of North India, which leaves scope for some local features. We usually begin in the garden, sitting on the wide stone circle for meditation round a great fire from which the new fire is taken and blessed, after the chanting of a Vedic hymn praying that the Lord will "take away our sin" and lead us to "the further shore of darkness." It is then carried in procession into the large open verandah where we have meals (the chapel is not large enough for the ceremonies). Instead of a candle we have a tall brass lampstand with four ties of wicks, forty in all. The top tier is lit, then after the Exsultet we sit for the readings. When we come to the renewal of baptismal commitment, each one lights a wick of the lamp, so that the "light of Christ" shines out more and more with each new flame. Those who have not made the commitment of baptism are also invited to renew their commitment to the values for which Jesus lived and died, however they would express it, by lighting a wick. At the end of the ceremonies we go to the chapel to "reinstall" the risen Lord in his sacramental presence as Guru of the Ashram with a striking prayer we borrow from the *Jñāneshwari,* which hails him as "the elephant in the garden of the dawn of knowledge," "who art the fulness of joy and destroyest forever all sin, the source of all creatures, who hast overcome the power of the serpent. . . . O God of love, who art the light in the house of thy devotees. . . ." At the end we sing the "Regina coeli" in Hindi, as we do every night, invoking the protection of the "Lord's mother," as our first Hindu member lovingly called her.

One of our most powerful experiences over the Easter Vigil arose, as so often happens, from an apparently chance occurrence: two young Jewish women staying with us asked if they might celebrate the Passover in the ashram on the Tuesday in Holy Week. They did it beautifully, with necessary adaptations for a vegetarian Indian household—grapes for wine and, to our astonishment, a small cross to represent the Paschal lamb. "After all, Jesus was the lamb of God," said one of them in casual explanation. The whole thing was reverent, relaxed, and profoundly moving. During it, one of the young women told us how the year before in her home, just before the Passover meal, they found that her uncle had hanged himself in the house, and her mother had to cut him down: she said, "That year it was not the Egyptians, but a Jewish family that mourned the death of a first-born son." She asked us to pause for a moment and pray "for everyone whom perhaps we have not loved enough." At the end, one of them turned to me and said, "Sara, would you like to tell us how your celebration this week is related to the Passover? I think this was its origin." Taken by surprise I simply said that though sometimes people think that Christians feel Christ has totally done away with the Jewish tradition, in reality we see him as the embodiment in our flesh of the love and compassion of God so beautifully spoken of in the readings we had just heard.

When I asked her if we might keep some of the unleavened bread left over for Maundy Thursday, and added, "You don't mind?" they answered quickly: "Why should we mind? You didn't mind us having the cross." This evening had a tremendous impact on us, not least because we knew how sharply they had been torn by the tension between their loyalty to their Jewish origins and their love for us: during their whole stay in the ashram I do not think they had once entered the chapel, and yet somehow the differences had been transcended in ways one would not have imagined possible.

This, however, was not the end. When we came to plan the liturgy for Thursday and Friday, we found that the sense of continuity with the Lord's own historical background was so powerful that we could not even envisage the possibility of readings or chants from the Hindu tradition except in our morning prayer: we had to take the Holy Week services straight from the missal, almost as though we were mesmerized. On Holy Saturday, however, to our amazement, we realized that the inhibition had vanished: we felt completely free to have introductory readings and chants from Indian sources at the Vigil. We therefore had a splendid trans-and-supra-cultural celebration.

Next day we sat down to reflect at leisure on this extraordinary experience we had had of feeling almost physically bound, and then free. What especially struck us was precisely the "bodily" aspect of the binding and the fact that we experienced it *as community.* Suddenly we realized that until his death, Jesus was bound by history and its limitations, but through his death and resurrection he had burst the bonds of space and time and could be recognized as not only Lord and Christ, but *Satpurusha,* the archetypal Man of Vedic tradition, in whom every member of the human race can recognize the truth of his or her own being.

A year or two after this we hit upon the inspiration of prolonging the Vigil by a week of *satsangs* beginning on the eve of Palm Sunday, several of which are devoted to the themes of the Vigil readings from the Old Testament, prayerfully pondered in the light of a parallel reading from Hindu scriptures and our own experience. This not only made it possible to go much deeper into the meaning of the Easter mystery, but also enabled us to feel free to introduce Indian readings in the earlier part of the Vigil itself which would help to make it more intelligible to our multi-religious household.

"This Man Is the Entire Universe": The Cosmic Dimension

The contemporary concern for the environment has reawakened Christians to an awareness of our cosmic setting which Hinduism has never lost. One year we took as our first reading for the Vigil the great creation hymn from the Ṛg Veda (10.90) which describes the coming into being of the whole cosmos through the willing sacrifice of the *Purusha* or *Satpurusha,* the archetypal Man: all the parts of the universe and the different classes of men came from different parts of his body. This life-giving death was also responsible, according to tradition, for the origin of the whole Vedic sacrificial system, for it was realized that if the process of diversification necessary for creation went on indefinitely, the result would be total disintegration of the *Purusha* and of creation itself. Therefore sacrifice was instituted by which every created being would return by a centripetal movement to its Source of true Self, acknowledging and renouncing the tendency to selfish individualism or false autonomy which would have destroyed the whole creation. As companion reading to this text we took Paul's famous passage on the one body and many members from 1 Corinthians, to drive home at micro-level, so to speak, that cosmic lesson of life born of self-sacrificing love, which is also the essential meaning of the paschal mystery.[11]

The juxtaposition of these texts was seen to have other very relevant implications: the Ṛg Vedic passage is often quoted today in the context of caste struggle as an example of brahminical oppression, composed, as the Dalits, or oppressed classes, claim, for the purpose of giving religious sanction to the unjust social structure. (In the hymn the brahmins come from the head of the Man, the other castes from progressively less "noble" parts.) An alternative interpretation, however, seems equally possible, namely, that whatever a person's social status, all are intrinsically worthy of the same respect because all come from the same Source which remains the inner dynamic principle and Self of all. The analogy of the body as presented by Paul makes this very clear, with the added insight into the necessity of diversity of function. (Obviously however this last point should not be used to justify any kind of oppression.)

We learnt from this reflection how cross-fertilization can bring out very vividly truths in both biblical and other texts which may have been dulled by constant repetition or, perhaps, may never even have been perceived at all, something which I have often verified personally in my interreligious contacts.[12]

MYTH AND HISTORY: LORD OF THE DANCE

The 1988 Vigil was epoch-making not only because it gave expression to the insight which settled the "universe of discourse" problem, but also because it gave powerful confirmation by the local "sensus ecclesiae" to this insight, which was the result of much long and painfully groping seeking for a way to explain, or rather present intelligibly, our faith-understanding of the Person of Christ in the Hindu context: how were we to explain our conviction that he is "God," or "son of God?" Finally I had begun to wonder if I was asking the wrong question: perhaps in India, where it is taken for granted by most people that, in ways not always clearly defined, "God" is the supreme reality in every person, it was more important to stress that Jesus was truly man, no mere celestial apparition, but bone of our bone and flesh of our flesh: *sarx egeneto*. (It is of course clear that the question of what we mean by the Incarnation has to be faced in both its aspects: I shall return to this later.)

I knew from my own hard-earned experience that, as I have already noted, for the devout Hindu it does not really matter whether Lord Krishna, for example, was a historical figure or not. (I had had a memorable encounter with a lady Swami in Rishikesh on this subject; fortunately I was fortified by memories of an earlier assurance by a Hindu pandit that this was indeed the case!) For us, however, the very foundation of our faith is that stark statement of the Prologue to John: "*ho logos sarx egento* — the Word *became* flesh." Prolonged reflection on this finally led to the breakthrough: the clue lay in the differing metaphysical status of the humanity of "Jesus who is called Christ" and the Hindu gods, which corresponds exactly to the difference between historical reality and myth in the technical sense. And yet, in Hindu tradition as in ours, it is human life and destiny that gives meaning to the whole of the coming-forth of creatures and their ultimate return to their Source. According to the Aitareya Upanishad, as we have seen, the supreme Reality, having brought this whole creation into being, "entered into creation for the sake of Self-realization," and according to the whole Vedantin tradition, this Self-realization can take place only in man. To speak of this process at all, names and forms are necessary, even for referring to the Name-less and the Formless, for which the least inadequate expression is "*neti, neti*—not this, not this." So we find the ultimate Mystery personified under three aspects as Brahma, the Creator, Viṣṇu, the Pervader and preserver, and Śiva, the Beneficent, who brings all things to their appointed end. In Śaivite tradition, however, Śiva is credited with all three functions; he is the dynamic inner Principle who animates the great dance of the Cosmos, and this is the meaning of his title of Naṭarāja or Lord of the Dance.

The Hindu gods, then are not historical figures, but *projections of the Hindu psyche* under the impact of a profound religious experience of that supreme Mystery which illumines everyone born into this world, of which the historically conditioned humanity of Jesus of Nazareth is the authentic and tangible Self-communication. Seen in this perspective there is no conflict, but rather a deep complementarity between, on the one hand, the Hindu myths as marvelous expressions of the experience of man-on-the-earth, who is part of the cosmos and yet ineluctably drawn beyond the visible world to the supreme Reality which he senses as present at the heart of every being and most intimately at the core of his own being; and, on the other hand, the Man who is born on earth as the historical expression of the *Satpurusha*, reliving in his own person, in a specific historical context, the mystery of the life-giving death of the *Purusha*. In so doing he offers to the whole human race a visible clue to the meaning of the human condition—the clue of self-sacrificing love exemplified in the myth of the *Purusha* and echoed by all the great spiritual teachers of India, as true of all times and places, for in the end they all come to the same conclusion—the self must die that the Self may live in all.

At the 1988 Vigil, in view of the long preparation of the *satsangs,* we had as the only readings before the New Testament ones the whole of the Katha Upanishad and Psalm 71. In the Katha Upanishad the boy Nachiketas is kept waiting for three days and nights outside the house of Yama, the Lord of death. As amends for this discourtesy, he is offered three boons. The third, which Yama is very reluctant to grant, is to know the secret of the ultimate goal of human existence, the meaning of human life. Yama finally yields and tells him of the two paths of life that lie before man for his choice with their very different ends, and of the

> one Ruler, the supreme Self, that is in all things—who transforms his own form into many. Only the wise who see him in their own souls attain eternal joy. . . . "This is That"—thus they realize the ineffable supreme joy. How can "This" be known? Does he give light or does he reflect light?
>
> There the sun shines not, nor the moon, nor the stars; lightnings shine not there, and much less earthly fire. From his light all these give light, and his radiance illumines all creation. (Kath. Up. 2.2.12–15)

Psalm 71 foretells the coming on the earth of a Man who "shall save the poor when they cry, and the needy who are helpless. He will have pity on the weak, and save the souls of the poor, for to him their souls are dear. May his name be blessed for ever, and endure like the sun. Every tribe shall be blessed in him, all nations bless his name." So we moved from the cosmic Upanishadic vision of "the human predicament," as Thomas Hobbes called it, to the more concrete earthbound perspective of the psalmist, and came to the threshold of the Easter proclamation of the "word made flesh" as the Man "who underwent death, and is alive to endless ages, and holds the keys of death and the underworld."

It seemed to us that this man could indeed be called "Lord of the Dance," for in his own life, death, and resurrection he visibly personifies the hidden rhythm of the Creator Spirit at work in us and in our confused and torn-apart world, bringing all things to their consummation in him. Throughout the Vigil a small, very beautiful image of the Naṭarāja stood at the base of the great Paschal lamp, gleaming in its light.

Not only did we ourselves feel that this had been a very powerful and decisive celebration: we received unexpected confirmation of this from an extremely intelligent and spiritual young Hindu who is a member of our wider community but had never before been with us for Easter. He spontaneously offered me "feedback." We discussed the choice of readings, and he agreed with the thinking behind the choice, namely, the distinction between Hindu gods and Jesus as one of myth and history. He added that there is something in the Gospel which India badly needs, namely, the selfless giving of life in service for others. He concluded by remarking that he fully agreed with another young Hindu who had been present that this had been "a thoroughly *Hindu* celebration!"

THE VIGIL *SATSANGS*

The prolongation of the Easter Vigil by a week-long series of leisurely *satsangs* has provided a unique opportunity for prayerful pondering by a cross-section of the human race on the mystery of human existence in the light of the death and resurrection of Jesus and vice versa. While the Vigils themselves are profoundly prayerful experiences, the *satsangs* also are extremely meditative: there is no formal discourse, simply spontaneous response to the readings and to each other's insights, but here also among ourselves we had to find some way of overcoming the "universe of discourse" problem, in view of our great variety of backgrounds. I found that my own familiarity with the advaitin tradition and considerable experience of introducing groups of students, seminarians, and others to the Upanishads was an invaluable help, for I have realized more and more what a fundamentally human document the Upanishads are. They illumine and corroborate the inner experience of men and women today because they spring from the absolutely primordial experience of *being* which lies dormant within each one of us, only waiting to be awakened into consciousness. I am sure that the clue to relating the death and resurrection of Jesus to the life of every other member of the human race lies here. We need to be able to transcend the limitations of his particular historical circumstances so that he stands revealed as not only a man, however great and good, but Man, the archetypal *Purusha* of whom every other human can cry: "*So'ham! So'ham! I am he!*"

CREATION: "NATURE" AND "GRACE"

In this perspective it seems significant that what strikes me every year as we consider the biblical and Hindu creation myths is the immediate response awakened in each group by the stress in the Hindu texts on the immanence of God, or the supreme Mystery in creation. This abiding presence of the Source or Principle of our being as Ground and Self of our limited selves is of course in perfect harmony with Christian creation theology, but it seems to come across much more powerfully through the Hindu texts. The Kena Upanishad in which the disciple suddenly comes to the awareness of the mystery of his own being and activity almost invariably arouses a profound sense of recognition in modern listeners: "Who sends the mind to wander afar? Who first drives life to start on its journey? What impels us to utter these words? Who is the spirit behind the eye and the ear?—It is the Ear of the ear, the Eye of the eye and the Word of the words, the life of life and the Mind of mind. . . . What cannot be thought by the mind, but that whereby the mind can think: know that alone to be Brahman, and not what people here adore" (1.1–2, 6). This seems to make much more sense to most people than talk of a God "up (or out) there," though it is not difficult to get them to realize that all such spatial categories are relative in character and dependent on our bodily nature: God is ultimately "neither within nor without" in spatial terms, though if we remember this, it is legitimate for us in our earthbound condition to speak of him as both.

We sometimes have to disentangle the theological and scientific approaches to the question of the origins of the universe, and we still encounter the occasional fundamentalist, but most often what rivets people is the sense of immediacy in the Upanishadic texts, a sudden awareness of "me" held in being "now," rather than a retrospective glance at something that happened on a cosmic scale in a remote and almost mythical past.

With regard to nature and grace, I have wondered for a long time whether we should not speak much more explicitly of grace or "justification" as a state or category of being, and in terms of the awakening of a latent capacity present in us by the very fact of our creation. Aquinas does in fact speak of a *potentia obedientialis* or capacity for response to an initiative of God that calls us beyond the range of our merely human powers. The usual way of speaking of baptism as though God or the Spirit or "sanctifying grace" "came in from outside," as it were, really makes very little sense in terms of the creation theology outlined above, or, in the last analysis, in terms of that of St. Thomas himself. It does however make very good sense, in relation to the understanding of the human person in terms of the *kośas* or "depths of interiority" described in my last lecture,[13] to speak of a new and progressively developing capacity for awareness of Ātman-Brahman, or God, as the Self of my own self, the prompter from within of every thought, word, and deed, without prejudice to the autonomy and freedom of my person (for, as Aquinas, says, freedom itself requires a cause), but rather strengthening and perfecting it so that the created being or "self" becomes more and more transparent to its Ground.

This seems to agree with the teaching, enshrined in Genesis and spelt out by traditional theology, to the effect that man and woman in the beginning had within them a latent capacity for defect which did not constitute a positive defect until it was actualized by a deliberate act of choice, and also a latent capacity for self-transcendence, or relating to and sharing in the blissful Self-knowledge of the Power that brought the human race into being. This latter capacity was partially activated from their creation, and for as long as their choices were in harmony with it,[14] but went into abeyance upon their conscious and deliberate preference of a lesser good. The whole of Hindu tradition agrees with biblical teaching that man, left to his own powers, cannot put an end to the state of abeyance. There is also general agreement that help to overcome it is forthcoming, with varying opinions as to the degree of cooperation to be expected from the individual human being. This approach has found considerable acceptance in the *satsangs*, as it seems to avoid the danger of dichotomizing "nature" and "grace" and reducing them to abstraction with little relevance to daily living. To speak of becoming more fully what one potentially is seems much nearer the mark.

Sin

The question of what went wrong with creation, and specifically with man, always evokes a lively discussion. Something clearly *is* wrong with all of us, and Hindu as well as biblical tradition is convinced of it. Indeed, the whole human race seems to have shared the conviction that initially "God made man right," so that his history began with a "Golden Age" that was somehow vitiated, since when things have gone from bad to worse, in spite of scientific and other relative forms of progress. What emerges clearly from the Genesis myth of the fall is that man's troubles are the result of his refusal to accept his proper status in the universe, that is, a rejection of right order.

It used to be said quite often by Christians that Hinduism had no clear conception of sin. I doubt if this thesis could be sustained today. As will be clear from what I have said so far, I am personally convinced that the Hindu equivalent of original sin is *avidyā*, or ignorance, understood as the tendency to err connatural to human beings, whose limited mode of existence always carries within itself by definition the possibility of failure. Essentially this is an existential kind of ignorance, a tendency to absolutize relatives, and most disastrously to absolutize the individual ego, so that it is substituted for the *Aham* of the great formula of liberation: *Aham brahmāsmi!* I am Brahman!" This of course is complete illusion and total destruction. So Yama, the Lord of death, says to the boy Nachiketas: "Abiding in the midst of ignorance, thinking themselves wise and learned, fools go hither and thither, like blind led by the blind. What lies beyond life shines not to those who are childish or careless or deluded by wealth. 'This is the only life, there is no other,' they say, and so they go from death to death" (Kaṭh.Up. 2).

Exploring these ideas, we have wondered whether the myth of the Golden Age cherished by the human race could not more convincingly be explained as a *projection behind us* of the dream of a perfect humanity and blessed state of existence for which we all long and however erratically strive. If so, it would be more appropriate to speak of an Ascent rather than a Fall of man, allowing, however, for the cumulative effect of *avidyā*-in-action on the condition of human society as a whole, as well as the development in many fields, partial but real, that has marked our history. This would seem more in harmony with the evolutionary view of the universe, which can no longer be simply written off, and so would offer a more satisfactory contemporary paradigm for our generation than the old one, without doing violence to its essential message. Indeed, it would help to eliminate some of its problems, not least that of the defacing of the image of God the Father, which has suffered so much from juridical theologies of salvation: it would no longer be necessary to hold that "God is a God of mercy and compassion *because* Jesus died."

I know that when some years ago the Dutch theologian Piet Schoonenberg offered a theology of original sin on somewhat similar lines, it was not well received in ecclesiastical circles, but perhaps this question needs to be looked at again in the light of the beliefs and experience of the human race as a whole and ongoing discoveries in relevant fields of knowledge.

What Think You of Christ? Whose Son Is He?

The person of Jesus and his role in human history has naturally taken much of our attention at *satsangs*. I have written a good deal about this elsewhere,[15] and will therefore mention here only what seem to me to be some of our more significant insights.

I have found Śaṅkarācārya extremely illuminating when grappling with the question of "Who is Jesus?" in the Indian context. The Questing Beast's problems with Chalcedon, or at least with the way in which its teaching of "two natures in one person" was commonly presented, led me to ask whether the concepts of *tādātmya* and *ananyatva* might not offer a more satisfactory formula. The Prologue to John's Gospel seemed to confirm this in the passage I have already quoted more than once—"The word *became* flesh." In other words, there was nothing in the man Jesus that was not Self-communication of God. He was, says the Letter to the Hebrews, "like us in everything but sin"—therefore there was and could be nothing in his humanity to distinguish him from us but the totality of its transparency and consequent obedience to God, a transparency which could do nothing to diminish his freedom as a human being, but on the contrary constituted and perfected it. There is no shadow of dualism here: limited though it necessarily was by the very fact of his being an individual man at a specific place and point in history, within those limitations his humanity was the fully human Self-expression of the Word in our nature, not a glove-puppet or microphone for the Word.

This formulation seems to safeguard not only the reality of his human nature, but also the unity of his person and the transcendence of his Godhead. The crux of the whole problem of expressing our theological understanding of the incarnation is obviously a question of relation: how can a Godhead which can undergo no change whatever be united with a humanity which has to be devoid of any differentia which would make it less fully human than that of any other member of the human race? "Fully God and fully man," says the Christian profession of faith. The non-reciprocal relation of *ananyatva*, a dependence so radical that the dependent reality cannot for a moment exist or act apart from its inner cause or Ground, which remains on its side wholly untouched by the relation, eliminates this difficulty completely. We obviously have here a particular and privileged instance of the relationship established by the primordial act of creation. There was in the man Jesus no tendency at all to claim a false autonomy, no shadow of *avidyā*: "First-born among many brethren," "like us in all things but sin," he could say with a depth of truth no other man could ever claim: "he who sees me sees the Father."

By the same token he is also the perfect paradigm of man's relation to God: wholly *ab alio* and *ad alium*, "from the Father and to the Father," the complete antithesis, especially in the freedom of his "obedience unto death," of man in revolt from God.

The most burning question about Jesus in the Hindu context, however, remains that of his "uniqueness"—the Christian claim that he is "the only way to salvation." This is something Hindus simply cannot understand. Perhaps it is time to ask ourselves what the Spirit is saying to the Churches through this total incomprehension.

"No One Comes to the Father but by Me"

I must confess that I was somewhat startled to read in a very appreciative review of my book *Lord of the Dance* in the journal of the Sri Ramanashram, Tiruvannamalai, that "Ms. Sara Grant's is a refreshing perception that is willing to consider any claim that Christ is the unique saviour as an intolerable narrowness, incompatible with the spirit of Christ's own Gospel." What I had actually said was that "the very foundation of one's Christian faith can suddenly appear to be threatened when one experiences for the first time . . . the impact of the advaitin experience, serenely incarnate perhaps in a gently and obviously saintly man ('the fruits of the Spirit are charity, joy, peace, patience . . .') who has scarcely heard of Christ or who regards him as a great teacher, *but considers any claim that he is the unique saviour as an intolerable narrowness incompatible with the spirit. . . .*" This is indeed the honest opinion of probably every sincere Hindu or member of any other faith, and yet from the beginning the universal salvific role of Jesus has been an integral part of Christian faith, and theologians have exerted themselves down through the ages to explain it convincingly. This has not always been easy. Karl Rahner's thesis of "anonymous Christians" met with considerable criticism, being regarded, unfairly it would seem, as a surrender to humanism,[16] and today we find a number of theological writers apparently willing to allow that Christ is the saviour for Christians, the Buddha for Buddhists, and so on. I do not think there can be any simplistic and piecemeal solution: certainly in an advaitin perspective one would feel obliged to safeguard both the ultimate unity of mankind's final destiny and the validity and variety of actually existing insights and ways of pursuing that ultimate goal. There must surely be some way of reconciling the fundamental Christian conviction that "Christ died for all men" and is in some very true sense for each one "way, truth, and life" with the obvious fact that millions of human beings who have never heard of him have found in the teachings of the *rishis*, the Buddha, the Prophet Muhammed, and other great and good men inspiration and guidance for leading lives that have flowered into manifest holiness. Faced by these facts, it is indeed difficult not to feel that one is exhibiting intolerable narrowness when one insists that "Jesus is the only way."

A Clue

The Prologue of John provides a clue to the relation between Jesus and the other religious and spiritual traditions of the human race when it speaks of the Word of Self-communication of God who "became flesh" as Jesus, as "the true Light illumining everyone born into the world." This is said of the Word without any explicit reference as yet to the incarnation, yet it is obvious that whatever truth and goodness the Word communicated to those other traditions cannot possible be alien to Jesus, and openness to them does indeed flow from commitment to him, as Dr. M. M. Thomas said. I think, however, that with the immense horizons opening up to us today through the coming together of cultures and religion and the discovery of worldviews quite different in many respects from our own, we have to envisage much more radical possibilities than a simple acknowledgment of this. Here it seems relevant to recall the remark from the Vatican II Decree on Ecumenism about the "continual reformation of which the Church always has need as she goes on her pilgrim way, insofar as she is an institution of men here on earth . . . even in the way that Church teaching has been formulated (to be carefully distinguished from the deposit of faith itself)" (no. 6). Our presentation of the theology of salvation would seem to be one of the areas where such reformulation is most urgently called for, and this not only for the sake of those of other faiths.

In the Indian context especially, I think we need to recover in our Christology the cosmic and theocentric vision of the early Church, for the loss of which reaction to the Arian heresy was no doubt largely responsible: the Father and the Spirit withdrew into the shadows.[17] The former only too often assumed the image of the stern and demanding judge, to be appeased only by the death of an innocent man, his own Son, and Jesus was left to carry the whole burden of redeeming the world, including somehow making salvation accessible to his fellow-members of the human race who would never hear of him through the teaching of his disciples.

If we go back to the origins and, accepting the complementarity of biblical and non-biblical scriptures, seek for the roots of a common vision, we may find our Christian faith immensely and unexpectedly enriched.[18] To anyone interested in such an adventure I would suggest as starting point the three following passages from the Chāndogya Upanishad, the Prologue of John, and the Ṛg Veda.

The Word (*Vac*) is truly greater than name. The Word in fact makes known the Rig Veda, the Yajur Veda, the Sāma Veda and the Atharva Veda as the fourth, the ancient lore as the fifth, the Veda of Vedas, the ritual for ancestors, calculus, the augural sciences, the science of the signs of the times, dialectics, ethics, political science, sacred knowledge, theology, knowledge of the spirits, military science, astrology, the science of snakes and celestial beings. (It also makes known) heaven and earth, wind and space, water and fire, the gods, men, beasts, birds, grass and trees, all animals down to worms, insects and ants. (The Word also makes known) what is right and wrong, truth and falsehood, good and evil, what is pleasing and what is unpleasing. The Word indeed makes all this known. Meditate on the Word. (Chānd.Up. 7.2.1)

In the beginning was the Word, and the Word was relation to God and the Word was God. He was in the beginning in relation to God. All things came into being through him, and apart from him nothing whatever came into being of all that came to be. In him was life, and the life was the light of men, and light shines in the darkness and the darkness has not overpowered it. . . . The Word was the true light that illumines every human being coming into this world. He was in the world, the world that came into being through him, and the world did not know him. He came to his own place, and those who were his own did not accept him. But to whomever did accept him he gave power to become children of God, to those who believed in his name. They were born not of blood, nor of the will of the flesh, nor of the will of man, but of God. And the Word became flesh, and pitched his tent among us, and we saw his glory, such glory as the only son receives from his father, full of grace and truth. (John 1:1–5, 9–14)

> What being I am I do not know:
> I wander secluded, weighed down by my mind
> When the First-born of Truth has come to me
> I became a sharer in that self-same Word.
>   (Ṛg Veda 1.164.37)

Though in the passage from the Chāndogya Upanishad *Vac* is taken primarily in the sense of human speech, in the Vedic tradition as a whole *Vac* is ultimately equated with Brahman as Word or utterance and is said to be "the speech of speech" (Kena Up. 1.2), "the womb of the universe," for "by that word of his, by that Self, he created all this, whatever there is" (Ś. B. 10.6.5.5). Even here these undertones can, I think, be sufficiently clearly discerned to justify the parallel with John.

We should also bear in mind the parallel between the Word and the *Purusha* or *Satpurusha* already spoken of, the archetypal Man, the "inner cause" of every human person, expression of the unique and indivisible mystery of Ātman-Brahman. The *Purusha* is an elusive and constantly-recurring theme of Vedic tradition, awakening echoes of the equally elusive and pervasive Man, or Son of Man, in the Judaeo-Christian scriptures, from "Adam" of Genesis to the "second Adam" and "whole Christ" of Paul and the "one like a Son of Man" of Revelation 1:9–16.

Against this backdrop we can now consider afresh the crucial question of how we are to understand the relation between the death and resurrection of Jesus and the salvation of all his fellow human beings. Traditional theology built upon the concept of efficient causality, most commonly interpreted in a juridical perspective[19]: the sin of mankind had to be atoned for by a sacrificial act, ideally as adequate as possible, and this act was performed by Jesus, so that the way lay open for all human beings to be restored to grace and reach their ultimate end by entering into the joy of their saving Lord. As already noted, the dynamics of this in the case of those who had never heard of Jesus, and therefore could not freely and consciously accept the offered gift, considerably exercised theologians, and the difficulty of defending the image of the Father as a God of love and infinite compassion was also almost insuperable: only a few years ago I heard a retreat preacher proclaiming that "*because* Jesus died, God is a God of love and compassion," whereas it is clearly the reverse that is true.

If on the other hand we consider the Word as the exemplar and dynamic archetype of all creatures, including man, another possibility presents itself. The Father, says Thomas Aquinas, "utters" the whole creation in his one Word, and every creature has within itself the thrust toward realization of its full potential, the teleological drive to become what it is, shot through in man with the promptings of "grace," for there has never been a purely "natural" man. The Word became flesh in the Judaic context, among a people who for centuries had been nomads and thought in terms of sacrifices of sheep and goats and other blood-offerings, and in terms of restitution in full for wrongs committed, somewhat on the lines followed by strict Islamic law even today. It was natural for them, and for Jesus himself, to interpret the death of Jesus in terms of the traditions of their own history and the scriptures born of their experience as a people. They had known God as lawgiver and judge to whom they were answerable in very concrete terms through the mediation of men, especially the prophets. It was therefore also natural for them to attribute the misfortunes of the human race to some primordial transgression. Yet perhaps the coming of the Word as a man among men to lead the whole creation back to the truth of its being could be understood and expressed differently in a different context without destroying the essential meaning of the original text, which remains normative in the sense that no alternative interpretation which is not faithful to its essential meaning can be accepted as authentic.

Here I have found inspiration in the figure of the *Satpurusha* and the understanding of "original sin" which evolved during our *satsangs:* the Word or *Satpurusha* in his human expression does not expiate a single and definitive primordial sin, but by meeting in his own life the consequences of man's accumulated willful actualizations of his ignorance, or tendency to absolutize relative values, and by his total selflessness and willing submission to the demands of human life as he experienced it, even unto death, he offered in his own person a living exemplar of man's return to his Source. This exemplar exerts a dynamic influence by the response it awakens in all who behold it, for in his death, even more than in his incarnation, he stands revealed as the personified expression of God's unconditional acceptance of and love for man, a personification which exerts the magnetic attraction of the final cause. As St. John of the Cross says, "it is for this love that we were created."

"There Is No Other Way to the Abode"

A question will still be raised about the vast numbers of men and women who never hear of Jesus. How do they relate to him and derive from him the life-giving energy to seek their true end, if even their juridical eligibility, so to speak, no longer holds? Here we have to turn to the Father and the Spirit. We have seen that by the fact of being "uttered" in the Word, an inner principle of finality is inscribed at the core of every being, and the Spirit who is the very union, essentially dynamic, of Father and Son," "ipsa unio Patris et Filii," in St. Thomas's phrase, urges and impels us to be faithful to that inner law of our being, which will, if we cooperate with it, make us in the end truly "sons in the Son." As "sons in the Son" both men and women grow progressively into the likeness of the archetypal Man, who as Jesus the Christ lived and died in a particular historical context yet nonetheless, in virtue of his being nothing but the faithful expression of the Archetype (nothing but communication of the Word, with no shadow of ignorance or egoism), remains forever in a very true sense the Way made visible for every human being—the way of self-sacrificing love even to death. Yet this is not the Way because he went it: he went it because it is the Way; not one of us can escape the necessity of going by it if we hope to reach the goal. We can all borrow the great cry of the sage of the Śvetāśvatara Upanishad:

> I know that great Purusha, shining like the sun beyond
>   darkness,
> knowing whom, a man passes beyond death.

There is no other way to the Abode.
I know him who is beyond age, who is the Self of all,
who goes everywhere, all-pervading.
Desiring true freedom, I run, I surrender, I go to him
who tells me by his light that I am the Self.

(Śvet. Up. 3.8,21)

As Paul would have said, "I live now no longer I, he lives in me" (Galatians 2:20).

This interpretation of the salvific role of Jesus in no way diminishes our Christian faith in the reality and value of his sacrificial death, which remains forever both the irrefutable proof of the love and compassion of God the Father and the efficacious and universally valid sacrament of man's self-gift to God and his fellow-men. As Paul says, whoever is conformed to Jesus in his death will likewise be conformed to him in the glory of his resurrection. Paul gives no indication that it is necessary to be conscious of this "conformity," and the parable of the Last Judgment in Matthew 25 clearly implies that it is not: "Lord, when did we see you. . . ?"

The final cause, said Aristotle, exercises its causality by the desire it awakens, the teleological pull it exerts. So the holy old Swamiji who was with us in Holy Week last year said slowly and with great conviction at the end of our Good Friday morning *satsang* on the death of the Lord: "Anyone who can stand before the cross and meditate on the death of Jesus, is Christ's man!"

Another old man, having listened to someone speaking about the Lord, stood up at the end and said: "Sir, I thank you. I have known him all my life, and now you have told me his name."

KURIOS, CHRISTOS, AND SATPURUSHA

As I was preparing the text of these lectures for publication, I came upon a review article by George Gispert-Sauch, S.J., of *Swami Abhishiktananda: His Life Told Through His Letters*,[20] which raises the question of the advaitin understanding of the resurrection:

> Once we take the stand of the advaita epistemology, and affirm that the world of history and plurality belongs to a *vyavahārika* (ordinary, everyday, relative) existence, and the world of Oneness and the Absolute to the *paramārthika* order (of supreme Reality), and affirm that the *vyavahārika* existence is inferior to the *paramārthika* and cannot be the Ultimate Truth, what value can we give to history, to the incarnation and even to the resurrection? Is the resurrection a "relative truth"? Or is it perhaps the expression of that passage from the *vyavahārika* perception of multiplicity in history to the *paramārthika* awareness that only I AM is real—the eternal I AM of Brahman which Abhishiktananda identifies with the history-oriented I AM of Exodus?

Gispert-Sauch concludes that "the basic problem for theology is therefore: What does the resurrection-experience at the heart of Christian faith really mean? Is it the illumination of the believer to see the glory of the Father in the life and death of Jesus? Or is it that paradoxical and foolish claim, unacceptable to all forms of gnosticism, that somehow the humanity of Jesus, transformed but real, has been exalted 'at the right hand the Father,' and that therefore history is now redeemed, ennobled, and 'impossibly' raised to the level of the *paramārthika?*"

While fully agreeing that the resurrection is an absolute crucial question for both Christian faith and advaita, I would myself approach the problem rather differently. As it is formulated here, it seems somewhat out of focus from an advaitin perspective; for Śaṅkara, the *vyavahārika* or created order of being could be understood only if it was seen in a relation of radical dependence on absolute Being, apart from which its existence is unthinkable. It is perfectly clear that the Eternal has no history, and as we saw in reflecting on the person of

Jesus, the incarnation poses in a peculiarly challenging form the question of the relation between the Eternal and the temporal. The rootedness of the resurrection in history, mediated to us through the faith-experience of the apostles and the early Church, and confirmed by the fact of the empty tomb— never formally adduced as evidence in apologetic argument, as critical exegesis has proved, and yet never controverted either[21]—is further corroborated by its immense repercussions on subsequent history down to our own time. It raises once more the profoundly metaphysical question of the relation between the Eternal and the temporal, between absolute Existence and created existence, in terms of the ultimate consummation of the latter.

From the advaitin point of view—at least from the point of view of the advaita of Śaṅkarācārya as I have understood it— it seems to be impossible for the *vyavahārika* world to be "raised to the level of the *paramārthika*" without vanishing altogether;[22] it also seems to be unnecessary from the Christian point of view. The *vyavahārika* world, including the humanity of Christ, is of its very nature constituted in being by a relationship of dependence on the *paramārthika* so radical that without this relation of "not-otherness" or "not existing apart from"— *anayatva*—it would not *be* at all. At present this is not a matter of either observation or experience to the human race in the normal run of things. Its sudden manifestation, whether to individuals at their time of "passing from this world to the Father," or at "the end of the ages" when "the Lord hands back the kingdom to the Father and God will be all in all," would seem to me to provide a perfectly adequate form of consummation for the universe which came into being in and through the Word, and finds its fulfilment through him by dying to the impulse to a false and self-destructive autonomy in the centripetal movement of the sacrificial return to the Source. If the precise manner of this reconstitution or resurrection of creation in the Word or *Satpurusha* eludes our mental grasp, this should not surprise us. Both Śaṅkara and our own tradition tell us that "reason has to abdicate any claim to self-sufficiency in the matter of supreme knowledge"; illumination here proceeds from the dark knowledge of faith, which is pure gift. Both *śruti* and scripture are silent.

In the last analysis I think that the most immediate contribution of the advaitin or *jñāni* to Christian theological reflection today should probably be not to devise yet another model for theologizing,[23] but rather to bring to the gatherings of theologians that piercing intuition into the fundamental structure of existence which constitutes the essence of advaita, and which of its very nature finds itself "contextualized" in every human situation. This intuition is born, as we have seen, not of mere reflection, though that too has its place, but of the grace of a profound experience of "that True outside of which no truth hath place" which can only be "prayed for to the exclusion of all else,"[24] in Śaṅkara's rather surprising phrase, and prepared for by a steady effort to bring one's whole life into harmony with that True.

There will always be different levels and styles of theologizing, some involving more profound academic study, some less, but all demanding that prayerful pondering within the heart, the experiential wisdom of the Spirit which gradually forms in us the mind and heart of Christ, and which characterized all the great theologians of the early Church in both East and West, and yet is given to the simplest lover of the Lord. At present, as a theologian friend wrote to me recently, "there are so many models of theology at large that often we are at cross-purposes in any dialogue." It is the peculiar gift of advaita to reconcile different points of view, not by canceling out one or the other, but by transcending both in a fuller synthesis, as the Questing Beast discovered. If we are to overcome our natural tendency, even in theological discussion, to fight to the death in defense of our own relative absolutes, we need to touch or be touched by the Absolute itself. Since we cannot exist without the security of some absolute, we are really incapable of letting our own conceptualizations go unless we have had this experience, however inchoate and fleeting, of the fullness of Being which is beyond all name and form, which both relativizes every created name or form and affirms it in its relative autonomy.

I said at the beginning of my first lecture that there is in every human being something of the *jñāni,* the *bhakti,* and the *karma yogi,* though in varying degrees. Each temperamental type or "way" has its own contribution to make to the Church and society at large. We all need each other, and in theological gatherings no less than in the rest of life the centripetal movement of convergence has to prevail over the tendency to diversification and self-assertion, lest we destroy the very richness of our diversity. The myth of the *Satpurusha* must be verified in us, as it was verified in the death and resurrection of the Lord himself, who knew more acutely than any other man that

> . . . the mind, mind has mountains; cliffs of fall
> Frightful, sheer, no-man-fathomed,[25]

for "At the end of all our knowing we know God as something unknown: we are united with him as to something wholly unknown," and yet "In every 'I' which I attempt to utter, his 'I' is already glowing."

Perhaps the specific vocation of the *jñāni* is to help humbly to keep that awareness alive in the Church.

NOTES

1. For my conviction that theological reflection is the birthright of every Christian, see my paper "The 'Viveka' within the Heart" in

Theological Education in India Today, ed. Felix Wilfred (Bangalore: Asian Trading Corporation, 1985), pp. 103–109.

2. It may seem paradoxical to say this in an age of proliferating fundamentalist groups until it is realized that these are for the most part the expression of a strong reaction of fear against the prevailing widening of horizons.

3. I was obviously not questioning the existence of God as a reality independent of the thinking mind.

4. The problem is not the intrinsic meaning of the term "Person" as originally understood in Christian theology, but the widely-accepted connotation given to that term today as a result of the development of psychology and psychotherapy, which stress the individuality and autonomy of the person, so that it is difficult to use the term in speaking of the Trinity without giving an impression of tritheism.

5. They produced a form of celebration of the Eucharist which was approved by the Anglican Church for use in India, but is now obsolete.

6. For other aspects see "Growth in Community: A Theological Perspective," in "The Way" Supplement, no. 62, Summer 1988, pp. 33–51, and several papers in *Lord of the Dance* (Bangalore: Asian Trading Corporation, 1987).

7. From the prayer we say just before the "Our Father" at the CNI Eucharist: "Father, we thank you for the union of mind and heart that you have created among us by the gift of your Spirit. With your Son we pray that full and visible union may soon be established among all Christians, as you will and by the means you will. Amen."

8. It was later renewed by our bishop when authority for liturgical experimentation was delegated by the CBCI to the bishops of each region.

9. Until 1988 we had a great Islamic scholar and Sufi in our community, Sister Arati K. Snow, R.S.C.J. Her death has left a great void.

10. The fact that modern biblical scholars recognize that some parts of the Gospels (e.g., the Infancy narratives) are myth in the technical sense and that some events, especially in John, have a symbolic significance only serves to emphasize this difference.

11. The relevance of this to the Eucharist is obvious, offering as it does to every successive generation the possibility of entering into the great movement of return and reintegration of the entire cosmos.

12. In 1975, during a talk at the *satsang* in the Sivananda Ashram, Rishikesh, apropos of the absolutely gratuitous character of creation

which seems to have baffled all philosophers, Hindu and Christian alike, I said that it seemed that in some mysterious way we had to conclude that in the last resort it was not we who thirsted for the Source, but the Source which thirsted to be thirsted for, adapting a sentence of Gregory of Nyssa. I added that this idea was there in both Hindu and Christian scriptures and quoted the Bhagavad Gītā, ch. 18:64–65, and St. John, "God loved us first." This made a great impact, and later in Allahabad, when I repeated the same thing to a young Sanskrit scholar, she said to me with shining eyes: "This is a *new* interpretation *we* are discovering!" I was especially happy with that "we."

13. See page 36–38.

14. According to traditional Christian theology, the preservation of harmony was itself a gift of grace.

15. See especially my paper "Shared Prayer and Sharing of Scriptures," in *Sharing Worship: Communicatio in Sacris,* ed. Paul Puthanangady, S.D.B. (Bangalore: National Biblical, Catechetical, and Liturgical Centre, 1988), pp. 459–481, and several papers in *Lord of the Dance.*

16. It too often seems to be forgotten that the fullness of humanity includes the spiritual dimension. "The glory of God is man fully alive," but the second half of that comment of St. Irenaeus is frequently omitted: "Life for man is the vision of God."

17. It is surprising how many Christians alienated from the Church have been encouraged to look again, and more closely, at the faith of their origins by discovering a community that is open to the truth of other Churches and other religions.

18. On the question of non-biblical scriptures in Christian worship, see *Research Seminar on Non-Biblical Scriptures,* ed. D.S. Amalorpavadass (Bangalore: National Biblical, Catechetical, and Liturgical Centre, 1974.)

19. Theory of "redemption" was no more satisfactory: "bought back" from whom?—hardly Satan.

20. See *Vidyajyoti: Journal of Theological Reflection,* vol. 54, no. 6 (June 1990): 300–304.

21. Cf. K. Rahner and Herbert Vorgrimler, "Resurrection of Christ," in *Concise Theological Dictionary* (London: Herder and Burns and Oates, 1965), pp. 405–408.

22. For Śaṅkara all created beings exist pre-eminently in Brahman as their Cause, but in that state are indistinguishable from Brahman;

so Aquinas says, "*Creatura in Deo est creatrix essentia*—the creature in God is the creative essence."

Śaṅkara has however an interesting passage, already quoted, on the manner in which "the knower of Brahman" enjoys created forms of happiness, which perhaps has a certain relevance here:

"The knower of Brahman enjoys all desires, all delights procured by desirable objects, without exception. Does he enjoy sons, heavens, etc., alternately, as we do? No, he enjoys all delectable things simultaneously as amassed together in a single moment, through a single perception, which is eternal, like the light of the sun, which is nondifferent from the essence of Brahman, and which we have described as Reality—Knowledge—Infinite. . . . He enjoys all things by that Brahman whose nature is omniscience. (Tait. Up. Bh. 2.1.1)

23. In a sense, of course, the advaitin cannot help offering this by his very manner of proceeding, but I do not think the establishing of a system should be his main preoccupation: his very raison d'etre is to point beyond all systems.

24. Muṇḍ. Up. Bh. 3.2.3.

25. Gerard Manley Hopkins, S. J., "No worst, there is none," 1885.

Abbreviations

Ait. Up.   Aitareya Upanishad

Ait. Up. Bh.   Śaṅkara's Commentary (bhāṣya) on the Aitareya
                    Upanishad

Bh. G. Bh.   Śaṅkara's Commentary on the Bhagavad-Gītā

Br. S.   Brahmasūtras of Bādarāyaṇa

Br. S. Bh.   Śaṅkara's Commentary on the Brahmasūtras

Bṛ. Up. Bh.   Śaṅkara's Commentary on the Bṛhadāraṇyaka
                    Upanishad

Chānd. Up. Bh.   Śaṅkara's Commentary on the Chāndogya
                    Upanishad

Kaṭh. Up.   Kaṭha Upanishad

Muṇḍ. Up. Bh.   Śaṅkara's Commentary on the Muṇḍaka
                    Upanishad

Ś. B.   Śatapatha Brāhmaṇa

Śvet. Up.   Śvetāśvatara Upanishad

Tait. Up. Bh.   Śaṅkara's Commentary on the Taittirīya
                    Upanishad

Upad.   Śaṅkara's Upadeśasāhasrī (A Thousand
                    Teachings)

99